"十三五"国家重点出版物出版规划项目
"中国传统文化体验课程"系列

Chinese Calligraphy

—The Art of Chinese Characters Textbook

——从造字艺术到书写艺术 课本

王晓钧　编著
By Xiaojun Wang

北京语言大学出版社
BEIJING LANGUAGE AND CULTURE
UNIVERSITY PRESS

© 2023 北京语言大学出版社，社图号 22039

图书在版编目（CIP）数据

中国书法 ：从造字艺术到书写艺术 ／ 王晓钧编著
. --北京 ：北京语言大学出版社，2023.4
ISBN 978-7-5619-6100-1

Ⅰ．①中… Ⅱ．①王… Ⅲ．①汉字－书法－对外汉语
教学－教学参考资料 Ⅳ．①H195.4

中国国家版本馆CIP数据核字(2023)第011081号

中国书法——从造字艺术到书写艺术
ZHONGGUO SHUFA——CONG ZAO ZI YISHU DAO SHUXIE YISHU

| 责任编辑： | 周 鹏 徐 梦 | 责任印制： | 周 焱 |
| 排版制作： | 李 越 | 封面设计： | 春天书装 |

出版发行：北京语言大学出版社
社　　址：北京市海淀区学院路 15 号，100083
网　　址：www.blcup.com
电子信箱：service@blcup.com
电　　话：编 辑 部　8610-82303670
　　　　　国内发行　8610-82303650/3591/3648
　　　　　海外发行　8610-82303365/3080/3668
　　　　　北语书店　8610-82303653
　　　　　网购咨询　8610-82303908
印　　刷：北京市金木堂数码科技有限公司

版　次：2023 年 4 月第 1 版	印　次：2023 年 4 月第 1 次印刷
开　本：889 毫米 × 1194 毫米 1/16	印　张：课本 12.25　练习册 13
字　数：321 千字	
定　价：88.00 元（含课本、练习册）	

PRINTED IN CHINA
凡有印装质量问题，本社负责调换。售后QQ号1367565611，电话010-82303590

序
Preface

呈现在读者面前的《中国书法——从造字艺术到书写艺术》一书是由长期在美国从事中国语言和文化教学与研究的美国西密歇根大学世界语言与文学系王晓钧教授撰写的。这是一部集汉字历史、造字艺术、书法赏析、书写指导为一体的教科书。全书由两部分组成，即汉字的造字艺术和书写艺术。该书从汉字起源、"六书"演变、线条结构、书法历史、文房四宝、"永"字八法、书法练习、艺术赏析等诸多方面入手，较为全面地介绍了汉字和书法艺术。全书内容翔实，循序渐进，引经据典，论证严谨。通过该书的讲解与呈现，学生们可以感受到中国古人的智慧，体会到中国书法的趣味和艺术的魅力。

这本书不仅为母语非中文的学习者介绍了汉字与书写知识，也为母语为中文的读者提供了再次研习汉字的机会。换言之，无论读者母语是否为中文，都可以从书中受益。该书的特点之一是：从讲解汉字如何而来到介绍如何用硬笔和毛笔写汉字，再到书法艺

Chinese Calligraphy—The Art of Chinese Characters is written by Dr. Xiaojun Wang, Professor of the Department of World Languages and Literature of Western Michigan University, who is an eminent scholar in the teaching and research of Chinese language and culture. This is a textbook that includes the history of Chinese characters, the art of character creation, the appreciation of calligraphy, and writing instruction. *Chinese Calligraphy—The Art of Chinese Characters* is composed of two parts: the art of character creation and the art of character writing. The author has discussed the origin of Chinese characters, the evolution of the "six categories", the lines and structures of characters, the history of calligraphy, the "four treasures" of the writing studio, the eight basic strokes of character *Yong*, the practice and appreciation of calligraphy and many others. This textbook comprehensively introduces the art of Chinese characters and calligraphy. Through the explanation and illustrations, students can feel the wisdom of ancient Chinese people, and appreciate Chinese calligraphy and its charm.

Not only does this textbook introduce Chinese characters and writing knowledge to non-native Chinese learners, but also provides an opportunity for native Chinese to study Chinese characters. In other words, readers can benefit from this textbook regardless of whether their native language is Chinese or not. There are several features in this textbook.

术赏析，为读者提供了完整的学习路径，力求从汉字的历史演变过程中梳理出汉字的特点与发展脉络。特点之二是：该书的内容涵盖了汉字的造字、结构和艺术性，三位一体，有助于书法课程的开设和讲授，能提高学生的审美素养，激发他们对中国文化的兴趣，从而从根本上打消汉字难学的观念，帮助学生树立学好中文的信心。特点之三是：汉字艺术的教学拓宽了汉字研究的视野，有助于学习者从多个角度了解中国文化。

我是通过使用王晓钧教授编写的《中国行——从传统走向现代》这本书与他相识的，后来又使用了他的《汉字与书法》一书。这些教材都体现了王晓钧教授深厚的学养，体现了他对中国文化与中国书法的深入研究，体现了他对这个领域教学的深刻思考与实践反思，以及他对所从事的跨文化国际传播事业的热爱与奉献。我早年在中国从事大学艺术教育，近 20 年来在美国从事中文及中国文化教学。汉字的造字艺术和书写艺术都是中国文化的瑰宝，汉字与书法教学也是国际中文教学重要的组成部分。学习者不仅可以提升中文的读写能力，还可以从中领略与欣赏中国古人融于自然的艺术鉴赏能力和创造能力，了解与感悟中国文化的源远流长与丰富多彩。

The first is the explanation of how Chinese characters came about, how to write Chinese characters with pens and brushes and the appreciation of Chinese calligraphy. It provides readers with a complete learning path, and strives to sort out the characteristics and development of Chinese characters from their historical evolution. The second feature is that the format from character creation to character structure and then to artistic form is very instructive to the establishment of calligraphy courses. It helps to enhance students' aesthetic appreciation and interest in Chinese culture. In return, it facilitates the students' learning, strengthens their confidence and eliminates the misconceptions that Chinese characters are too difficult to learn. The third feature of the textbook is that by learning the artistry of Chinese characters and writing system, students achieve a new perspective and deeper understanding of the multifaceted Chinese culture.

I first had an acquaintance with Professor Xiaojun Wang by adopting his textbook *China in View—From Tradition to Contemporary*, and later his book *Amazing Characters & Magic Brushwork*. These textbooks reflect his profound knowledge of and in-depth research on Chinese culture and Chinese calligraphy, his pondering and reflection on teaching and practice in this field, and his dedication and devotion to the cross-cultural communication career in which he is engaged. In the early years of my career, I taught Art Appreciation in a university in China. Since moving to the United States, I have been teaching Chinese language and Chinese culture for nearly twenty years. The art of character creation and the art of character writing are both cultural treasures of China. The teaching

非常感谢王老师与我们中文教学的从业者、中国文化的研究者及广大的学习者分享这部著作，分享博大精深的中国文化。《释名》中说："文者，会集众彩，以成锦绣。"研习中国文化和汉字艺术可以使我们的文化更加锦绣多彩。承蒙王老师不弃，邀我在卷首写上几句。我诚恳地把这本书推荐给国际教学界与中国文化教学界的同行们，希望更多的老师和学生从汉字和书法中体会艺术乐趣，提升审美修养，并终身受益。

刘　金

查菲学院

2021 年 4 月 28 日于美国洛杉矶

of Chinese characters and calligraphy is an essential part of Chinese teaching. Not only can learners improve their reading and writing abilities in Chinese, but also appreciate the art and creativity of the Chinese ancestors in harmony with nature, and understand the long history and richness of Chinese culture.

Thank you, Dr. Wang, for sharing this textbook with Chinese teaching professionals, researchers of Chinese culture and Chinese learners. Thank you also for sharing the profound Chinese culture. In *Shi Ming*, it says: "The 'script' is to gather all kinds of broad and vivid colors to create splendidness." Studying Chinese culture and the art of Chinese characters can deepen the richness of Chinese culture. I express my gratitude to Dr. Wang for inviting me to share my thoughts here. I sincerely recommend this textbook to my colleagues in the field of Chinese language and culture instruction. I hope that more teachers and students can experience the artistic fun from Chinese characters and calligraphy and enjoy the beauty around us in our daily life. This will be a lifetime benefit.

Dr. Jin Liu
Chaffey College
April 28th, 2021, Los Angeles, USA

编写说明
Author's Note

随着国际中文教育的兴起，中国文化的瑰宝——汉字与书法也引起了越来越多人的兴趣和关注。2009年，《汉字与书法》一书应运而生，由北京语言大学出版社编辑出版，深受广大学习者喜爱，一直作为教科书使用。"中国书法"也被很多大学设为选修课，每个学期选修这门课的学生都人数众多。究其原因，通过这门课，学习者不仅能学习世界上使用人数最多的文字，增强语言技能，而且能了解汉字的来源和结构，感受中国文化的魅力，同时也能从艺术的角度对汉字与书法有更进一步的了解。有鉴于此，我们根据多年的教学实践和师生反馈，对《汉字与书法》这部教材进行了全面的修订，从"造字艺术"和"书写艺术"两个层面来展示汉字的美学价值，揭开中国书法的神秘面纱，帮助学习者增强汉字的读写能力，掌握汉字的构造和书写规律，并让他们亲身感受中国汉字和书法的奥妙，领略中国书法的真谛。

对于第二语言学习者来说，学习中文最大的挑战，也是最让人感兴趣的事情之一就

Chinese characters and calligraphy, as Chinese cultural treasures, have attracted more and more people's interest and attention with the rise of international Chinese language education. In 2009, *Amazing Characters & Magic Brushwork* was edited and published by Beijing Language and Culture University Press. It has been used as the textbook and welcomed by users since then. "Chinese Calligraphy" has also been set up as one of the elective courses in universities, and there are a large number of students taking this course each semester. The reason is that, through this course, not only can learners learn the most populous written character in the world and strengthen their language skills, but also learn about the origin and internal structure of Chinese characters, and feel the charm of Chinese culture. They also have a better and deeper understanding of Chinese characters and calligraphy from the artistic perspective. In view of this, we have made a comprehensive revision of this textbook based on years of teaching practice and feedback from readers. The new textbook is aimed at unveiling the mystery of Chinese calligraphy by showing the aesthetic value of Chinese characters from the two aspects: the art of character creation and the art of character writing, so that it can help learners enhance their reading and writing abilities, master the structure of Chinese

是中文的书写系统。公元 100 年，最早的一部中文字典《说文解字》面世时，就已经收录了 9 353 个汉字。到了公元 1039 年，字典《集韵》出版时，收录的汉字已经增加到了 53 525 个。已有 5000 年以上历史的汉字，是世界上历史最长且最复杂的书写系统之一。它同时也是使用人数最多、最具有吸引力的一种文字。当今世界，使用汉字的人数已经超过 15 亿，主要分布在中国的大陆（内地）、台湾、香港、澳门以及日本、韩国和东南亚地区。

汉字的魅力之所以经久不衰，其原因包括两个方面：一方面是汉字本身，另一方面则是书法的作用。汉字的创造是神奇的，而如何书写汉字更是奇妙的。对大多数人来说，汉字的神秘不仅在于它的起源，而且也在于如何用艺术的形式来展示它内在的构造。事实上，汉字不仅是一种书面文字，其本身也是一种艺术。在汉字的背后潜藏着美学的基本原理。许多人都认为，中国书法就像是没有景物和色彩的图画、没有声音和音符的音乐、没有表演者的舞蹈、没有建筑材料的亭台楼阁。中国书法的美妙基于自然之美，充满平衡、和谐、动感、变化、活力和韵律。这些代表着所有纯正的艺术的真谛。

characters and writing rules, and appreciate the true meaning of Chinese calligraphy by experiencing the charm of Chinese characters and calligraphy.

One of the biggest challenges but also the most interesting things for second language learners to learn Chinese is the Chinese writing system. The earliest Chinese dictionary *Shuowen Jiezi*, published in 100 A.D. included 9,353 characters. By 1039 A.D., the number of the characters had accumulated to 53,525 in the dictionary *Ji Yun*. With a history of more than 5,000 years, Chinese character is one of the most oldest and complicated writing systems in the world. It is also one of the most popular and attractive characters. Nowadays it is actively used by over 1.5 billion people in China's mainland, Taiwan, Hong Kong, Macao, as well as Japan, South Korea, and Southeast Asia.

The attraction of Chinese characters is twofold: one is the construction of the character itself and the other is the beauty of Chinese calligraphy. The creation of characters is fascinating and the various ways to write them are exquisite. How characters were originally formed and how they have come to be presented in artistic handwriting are a mystery to most people. In fact, Chinese characters function both as a written language and as an art. General aesthetic principles underlie this art. Chinese calligraphy has been described as "painting without objects or colors, music without sounds or notes, dance without performers, and pavilions without building materials". The beauty of Chinese calligraphy is essentially the beauty of nature —balance, unity, motion, change, vitality and rhythm. It represents the true essence of all

编写这本教材的动因源于探讨外国学生学习汉字和练习书法之间的关系。十几年前，我们大学开设中文书法课的时候，市场上找不到可供母语为非汉语的学生使用的书法教材，而且中文汉字课和书法课也没有直接的联系。因此，本教材的目的在于从美学的角度来介绍汉字，并试图为这个领域提供一部兼具综合性和实用性的教学材料。我们在以下五个教学法方面进行了尝试，以求满足学生和教师的需求。

■ 把汉字学习和书法练习结合起来

汉字在西方有"东方魔方"的称号，这也是吸引西方人学习中文的主要原因之一。但是，当学习者尽力去记忆某个汉字的一笔一画时，他们往往忽略了这个汉字的内在美。因此，如果能引导他们看到每个汉字的结构所展示的艺术魅力，那么将对他们的汉字学习起到重要作用。当学习者懂得欣赏汉字的形体之美时，他们往往会乐此不疲地反复去读写这些汉字。当他们练习书法时，也会自然而然地分析每个汉字的内部结构。为了达到这个目的，本教材综合了有关汉字的基本知识和汉字的书写艺术。

genuine art.

What motivated me to work on this textbook was the relationship between learning characters and practicing calligraphy for foreign students. When we offered a course of Chinese Calligraphy decade years ago, there were no available calligraphy materials for non-native learners on the market and there was no connection between character learning and calligraphy training. Therefore, the purpose of this textbook is to introduce characters with an aesthetic approach, and provide an integrated and user-friendly textbook for this field. We have made the following pedagogical approaches to meet the needs of both students and instructors.

• Combining character learning with calligraphy training

The Chinese character has been nicknamed "the oriental mystical square" in the West. It is also the major attraction for many Westerners to learn Chinese. However, learners often ignore the beauty of the character when they try to remember each stroke of a character. Therefore, it is important for them to see the art that underlies each character's construction. It will motivate the learners to read and write the characters tirelessly if they appreciate the beauty of the character forms first. They naturally understand how a character is constructed when they practice calligraphy. For that purpose, the textbook has integrated the basic knowledge about characters with the aesthetics of character writing.

• Combining hard-tip calligraphy with brush calligraphy

Chinese calligraphy has been traditionally

■ 把硬笔书法和毛笔书法结合起来

传统上，中国书法一直被认为是用毛笔书写汉字、创造意境、表达情感的艺术。但是，现实生活中我们天天都在使用的是铅笔、圆珠笔或钢笔。在现代社会中，这些书写工具无疑比毛笔方便且普及得多。事实上，人们已认同并接受硬笔书法也是一种艺术。因此，本教材除了介绍硬笔书法外，还设计了很多练习，让学习者在使用毛笔之前先打好基础。

■ 把书法理论和书法练习结合起来

学习书法不仅要有基本的理论知识，同时还需要大量的练习。因此，本教材分为课本和练习册两个部分。课本介绍了有关汉字的笔画、笔顺、结构、书体、源流及书法欣赏等知识；练习册则提供了从笔画到部首、从单字到句章的训练，以及描摹、临帖等各种练习方法。为了便于学生和教师使用，课本每一章的后面都有根据讲授内容提出的思考题，可以作为家庭作业或课堂讨论的内容；练习册中则附有相应的参考答案。除此之外，教材中还设计了"书法习作"单元，通过提供建议和范例，引导学习者尝试创作独立构思的书法习作。学习者可以运用自己学到的书法知识和技能，结合对不同文化的解

considered the art of using a brush to create an artistic mood and express feelings. Today, however, we use pencils or hard-tip pens to write, as they have become more convenient and popular than brushes. In fact, hard-tip calligraphy is now considered and accepted as an art. Therefore, this textbook has introduced a hard-tip calligraphy section and designed many exercises for learners to work on it before they start to use the brush to write.

• **Combining theories on calligraphy with calligraphy training**

Learning Chinese calligraphy requires not only mastery of the basic theory, but also a lot of practice. Therefore, this series of textbooks has two volumes—Textbook and Workbook. The knowledge of the strokes, the stroke order, the construction, the styles, the origins and the appreciation of Chinese calligraphy is introduced in the Textbook. The step-by-step exercises on tracing, copying model works of strokes, radicals, characters, and a piece of calligraphic work are provided in the Workbook. There is a section of questions after each chapter in the Textbook that is based on the content of that chapter. These questions can be used as homework or classroom discussions. The answer keys are offered in the Workbook. In addition, the textbook has also designed a chapter for learners to work on a self-designed calligraphic project by providing suggestions and samples for learners to brainstorm. Learners can use their knowledge and skills on calligraphy and combine their understanding of different cultures in their brushwork, so as to bring their initiative and creativity into full play.

读和领悟进行书法创作，以提高书法学习的
积极性和创造性。

■ 把中国书法和中国文化结合起来

虽然中文书写系统看起来相当复杂，但是学起来却趣味无穷。其实，汉字并非只是古老的书写符号，它也是组成中国文化的要素之一，在中国人的文化生活中起着重要的作用。每个汉字都折射出了古代中国人的智慧和创造力，都包含着源远流长的中国文化的底蕴和深邃的哲学思想。本教材的目的之一就是把中文书面语和中国的哲学、艺术结合起来，从而给学习者提供综合性的学习材料以及相关活动的建议，使其对中国的书面语和文化艺术有比较深入的了解。

■ 把汉字书法和东方艺术结合起来

汉字与书法如影随形，相伴而生，源远流长。书法艺术来自汉字的造字艺术，反过来也影响了汉字的结构美和形体美。可以说，中国古人从第一个汉字的创造开始就有了对艺术的追求。中国汉字与书法之所以流传至今，日益兴盛，趣味无穷，令人陶醉其中，是与其奇妙的艺术魅力分不开的。正如表意文字不同于表音文字，东方艺术也不同于西方艺术，具有其自身的鲜明特点。汉字

- **Combining Chinese calligraphy with Chinese culture**

Although the Chinese writing system is quite complicated, it is also very interesting. In fact, the Chinese character is not just the symbol created in ancient times, but also is an essential element in Chinese culture. Chinese calligraphy plays an important role in the artistic life of the Chinese people. Every character reflects the wisdom and creative power of ancient Chinese people, and underlies the long and rich history of Chinese culture and philosophy. One of the purposes of this textbook is to combine Chinese written language with Chinese philosophy and art, and provide students with integrated learning materials and activities to help them have a deeper understanding of Chinese written language, culture and art.

- **Combining Chinese characters & calligraphy with Oriental art**

Chinese characters and calligraphy follow each other like shadows and appear like partners, which can be traced back a long time ago. The art of Chinese calligraphy comes from the artistic approach to creating Chinese characters, which in turn has promoted the artistry of Chinese characters. It could be said that the ancient Chinese have had the pursuit of art since the creation of the first Chinese character. The reason why Chinese characters and calligraphy can spread to the present, even more widely used is that their fantastic artistic charm. Just as ideographic writing system is different from phonetic writing system, Oriental art is also different from Western art. It has many distinctive features. Chinese characters and calligraphy are the root and the crystallization of Oriental art.

与书法是东方艺术之根，也是东方艺术的结晶。学习中国汉字和书法，为接触和了解东方艺术打开了大门。因此，本教材在介绍汉字的起源、笔画、笔顺和结构等基本知识时，也强调了汉字的自然美、结构美、寓意美，以及汉字所呈现的独特的线条造型艺术，力图把汉字和书法学习与培养学生的审美能力结合起来。正如西汉学者扬雄所说："书，心画也"，书写汉字如同用内心在绘画。民国高僧印光大师也曾说："字为世间至宝，能使凡者圣，愚者智，贫贱者富贵，疾病者康宁。"汉字与书法不仅承载着、传播着中国的文化艺术，而且本身就完美体现了人们对美的追求。我们可以通过教学来提升学习者的艺术情操。

本教材可供没有中文背景的学习者使用，每个对中国文字和书法感兴趣的人也都可以参考。因此，它不仅可以作为大学相关课程的教材，也可以供中学或周末学校、夜校的师生参考，还可以作为自学材料。希望本教材能够满足那些想在书法教学的同时进行汉字教学的教师和学生的需求。由于本教材主要是为母语为非汉语的读者编写的，因此书中并没有关于书法源流等方面的详尽介

Learning Chinese characters and calligraphy opens the door for understanding Oriental art. In order to combine the learning of Chinese characters and calligraphy with the cultivation of students' aesthetic ability, this textbook emphasizes the natural beauty, structural beauty, implied beauty of Chinese characters, as well as the unique line art presented by Chinese characters while introducing the origin, strokes, stroke orders and structures of characters. As scholar Yang Xiong in the Western Han Dynasty indicated: "writings are heart paintings". Writing Chinese characters is like drawing with the heart. Master Yin Guang, an eminent monk, once also said: "The characters are the treasures of the world, which can make an ordinary person a superman, make fools wise, make the poor rich and noble, and restore health to the sick". Chinese characters and calligraphy not only inherit and spread Chinese culture and art, but themselves perfectly embody people's pursuit of beauty. We can improve learners' artistic sentiment through teaching.

This textbook is designed for learners without Chinese background. Everyone who is interested in Chinese writing system and calligraphy can also use it. Therefore, it can be used not only for college courses, but also at middle schools, Sunday or evening schools or for self-instructional purposes. I hope that this series of textbooks can meet the needs of both instructors and students who want to teach and learn Chinese calligraphy while also teaching and learning Chinese characters. Since it is intended for general readers whose native language is not Chinese, I have focused on methodology of teaching and learning

绍，而是把重点放在中文作为第二语言教学的角度上。为了改进编写质量，欢迎使用者赐予中肯的意见或建议。

王晓钧

2021 年 6 月

Chinese as a second language and have not dealt in details with historical background of Chinese calligraphy. To improve the future editions of this series of textbooks, any criticisms or suggestions are welcome.

Xiaojun Wang
June 2021

目 录
Contents

UNIT ONE 第一单元

1

The Art of Character Creation 造字艺术

第一章　语言与文字
Chapter One　Languages and Writing Systems

1.1 文字的作用

　　什么是文字？简言之，文字是记录语言的工具，文字建立在语言的基础之上。因此，当讨论某种语言的文字时，首先要了解什么是语言。众所周知，语言是人类最显著的特征之一，也是人类最宝贵的财富。没有语言，就没有今天人类的文明，也没有人类的进步。任何一个正常人都具有一定的语言能力，任何一种生产活动和社会活动都离不开语言。语言是约定俗成的语音系统和语义系统，具有创造性，可以通过有限的音素和语素来表达无限多的内容。"我们经由语言创造世界，世界经由语言而产生。"（马尔·潘科斯特）尽管人类无时无刻不在使用语言，但是却很难给语言下一个十分准确的定义。语言到底是由什么组成的？文字是不是语言的一部分？人类为了达到交际的目的而使用语言，交际中离不开语音、词汇和语法。因此，语音、词汇和语法是构成语言的三大要素，缺少任何一个要素，人类便无法交流。据统计，目前世界上大约有 6500 种

1.1 The Functions of Writing Systems

　　What is the writing system? In short, writing systems have been created based on languages, and they have served as a tool for recording languages. Therefore, before discussing the writing system of a language, first understand what language is. As we all know, language is one of the most remarkable features of mankind and the most precious asset. Without language, there would be no human civilization and no human progress. Every normal person uses language. Any production and social activities are inseparable from language. Language is a conventional phonetic system and semantic system. Language becomes creative and can express infinite content through limited phonemes and morphemes. "We invent the world through language. The world occurs through language" (Mal Pancoast). Although human beings use language all the time, it is difficult to give an accurate definition. What is a language composed of? Is written text a fundamental part of a language? Human beings use language to communicate, and pronunciation, vocabulary and grammar are inseparable from communication. Therefore, language must include these three elements. Without any one element, human beings cannot communicate with each other. According to statistics, there are currently

语言（其中有 2000 种语言使用人数很少，每种语言的使用人数低于 1000 人）。在这 6500 种语言里，有 3866 种语言有自己的或借用的书写系统，而其余的 2634 种语言则没有文字。可见，书写系统并不是构成语言的基本要素，没有文字的语言也是语言，不会书写的人也可以用口语进行交际。语言的书写系统固然重要，但并不是语言必需的组成部分。

有文字的语言可分为口语和书面语。从语言的发展历史来看，无论哪种语言，都是先有口头语言，然后才逐步建立起书写系统的，口语一定先于书面语。虽然文字最初的作用只是用来记录口头语言，但是它解决了有声语言在时间上和空间上的局限性。没有文字的语言就没有书面的记录。如果这种语言未能口耳相传，一代一代流传下去，那么它就会像从来没有存在过一样，它所承载的文化和历史也会随之消失。由于文字可以记录思想和事件，所以不仅使文化和历史得以传承，而且也使人脱离了有声语言转瞬即逝的阶段，打破了距离和地域的限制，大大提高了交流的效率，促进了人们思维的发展，加快了知识和文化的传播。可以说，文字的发明是人类最

about 6,500 languages in the world, 2,000 of which are used by less than 1,000 people each. Of all 6,500 languages, 3,866 languages have their own or borrowed writing systems, the remaining 2,634 languages have no written text. It is thus clear that the writing system is not a basic element of a language. Languages without writing systems are still languages; those who can't write still communicate using spoken language. The writing system is important, but not a necessary component of a language.

Languages with writing systems can be divided into spoken and written languages. Historically, the writing system has always developed gradually after its spoken counterpart appears. The spoken language always precedes the written language. Even though the writing system was originally intended to record spoken language, it also made up for the limitation of the verbal language in transcending time and space. There would be no record of the language without written text. If the language is not passed down, the culture and history that it carries would disappear as if it had never existed. The writing system can record thoughts and events, so not only can culture and history be passed down, but the verbal language can be retained despite its limitations of distance and geographic location. The writing system also offers more efficient communication, promoting scholarly thought, and accelerating the dissemination of knowledge and culture. It could be said that

伟大的成就之一，是从原始社会过渡到文明社会的标志，是人类文明发展的里程碑。

文字系统实际上是一套符号系统，用来代表和记录口语中的语音和语义。原始文字的出现可以追溯到大约 5000 年前。关于文字的起源，有多种不同的解释。有的学者认为是宗教促成了文字的产生，也有人认为文字是适应早期商务记录的需求而产生的。这些说法都需要通过考古和学术研究来证实。古希腊哲学家柏拉图（前 427—前 347）在他著名的对话集《斐德罗篇》中曾谈到来自古埃及的关于文字的神话。据说，一个名叫修斯的神发明了文字，他非常激动地把这一发明告诉了古埃及王泰莫斯，认为他的发明能使埃及人增强记忆力并变得更加聪明，是记忆和智力的万能药。埃及王并不赞同这个说法，他认为文字虽然能让人把信息存在纸上，但并不能保证增强人们的记忆力，读者也无须用脑思考，因而不是真正的智慧。虽然这个传说无法证实，但它却如实反映了文字的作用。毫无疑问，人类需要把重要的信息详细地记录下来，文字的产生是跟人类实际的需求紧密相连的。正如亚

inventing writing systems is one of mankind's greatest achievements. The writing system is a symbol of the transition from primitive society to civil society and it is a milestone in the development of human civilization.

The writing system is actually a set of symbolic system used to represent and record pronunciation and semantics in spoken language. The earliest appearance of the writing system can be traced back to about 5,000 years ago. There are many different explanations for the origin of the writing system. Some scholars believe that religion promotes the generation of the writing system, while others believe that the writing system was created in response to the need for early business records. These claims have yet to be confirmed by archaeological and academic research. The ancient Greek philosopher Plato (427 B.C.–347 B.C.) spoke about the myth of writing system's origin from ancient Egypt in his famous dialogue set *Phaedrus*. It is said that a god named Theuth invented the writing system and was very excited to tell his invention to the ancient Egyptian King Thamus, believing that his invention would enable the Egyptians to enhance memories and cleverness—a panacea for memory and intelligence. Thamus did not agree with this statement. He believed that the text allowed people to put information on paper without committing to memory, and since the readers did not need to think, it was not true wisdom. Although none can confirm the myth's authenticity, it faithfully reflects the role of the

里士多德（前384—前322）所说："话语代表人们的思想，而文字代表话语。"

原始文字是人类用来记录特定事物的工具。可以肯定，各种语言的文字在发展早期都是简化的图画形式，人们把各种约定俗成的记号留在岩石、金属、树皮等物体上。这些早期的文字都属于图画文字，可以大致分为两类：一类是表意文字，即以形表意；另一类是表音文字，即以形表音。表意文字与语音没有什么联系，而是用字形来反映字义，比如早期的中国文字。尽管人们生活在不同的方言区，发音不同，但字义却是基本相同的。表音文字则跟字义没有必然的联系，它通过图画文字来标注语音。比如古埃及文、罗马文、拉丁文等，都经过原始图画逐渐发展为语音符号，即用不同的字母分别代表不同的音，不同的音拼在一起形成音节，成为记录语音的表音文字。

从原始文字的构成和发展可以看到，任何语言的文字都具有三个组成要素：形、音、义。三者之间关系不同，构成的文字也不同。人们在书写的时候，用不同的方式把所书写的符号和语音、语义联系起来，由此创造出不同的书写系

text. There is no doubt that human beings need to record important information in details, and the generation of the writing system is closely linked to the practical needs of human beings. As Aristotle (384 B.C.–322 B.C.) puts it, "Speech is the representation of the mind, and writing is the representation of speech".

Primitive text was a tool for human beings to record a particular thing. Text in various languages began as simplified forms of pictures; people left commonly accepted symbols on rocks, metals, barks, and so on. These early writing systems belong to the pictorial text and can be roughly divided into two categories. One is the ideographic script, that is, the form is expressed, and the other is the phonetic script, which correlates a symbol with a sound. The ideogram has nothing to do with the sound. Rather, the ideograph's glyph can be linked to the meaning of the character, such as the early Chinese characters. Although people live in different dialect areas and their pronunciations are different, the written characters' meanings remain the same. The phonetic script is not necessarily related to the meaning of the character; rather, the sound is marked by the pictorial text. For example, ancient Egyptian, Roman, and Latin have developed into phonetic symbols through this process. Different letters represent different sounds, which combine to form a syllable, culminating into a phonetic transcription to record sound.

We can see from the composition and development of the primitive text,

统。有些文字注重拼写与读音的关系，有些则把书写符号和意思紧密联系起来，还有的文字既有表音的部分，也有表意的符号，可以称为意音文字。虽然世界上3000多种语言有自己的书写系统，但是根据各种文字中形、音、义之间组合关系的不同，文字基本上可以分为三种类型：（1）音素文字，如拉丁字母、阿拉伯字母、西里尔字母、梵文字母（图1-1）等。（2）音节文字，一般一个字符代表一个音节，如日文的音节符号——假名。（3）意音文字，或称"语素文字"，一般一个字代表一个语素。这种文字既有表示意思的部分，又可能有表示声音的部分，如中文使用的汉字。

图1-1　中国正觉寺有一块用梵文书写的牌匾
Figure 1-1　There is a plaque written in Sanskrit in Zhengjue Temple, China.

　　汉字是记录汉语的书写符号系统，是世界上最古老的文字之一。汉字的出现和使用对中华文明产生了重大的影响，

the composition and development of any language's text have three components: shape, sound, and meaning. Different relationships between shape, sound and meaning make different characters. When people write, they use different ways to connect written symbols with speech and semantics; therefore, the creation of written systems differs from each other. Some characters focus on the relationship between spelling and pronunciation, others closely relate writing symbols to meanings, and some characters have both parts of the phonetic and ideographic symbols which can be called ideographic characters. Although more than 3,000 languages in the world have their own writing systems, they can basically be divided into three categories according to the combination of shape, sound, and meaning in various writings: (1) phonetic writing systems, such as Latin alphabet, Arabic alphabet, Cyrillic letters, Sanskrit letters (Figure 1-1), etc.; (2) syllabic writing systems, in which one character generally corresponds to one syllable, such as Japanese syllabic script—kana; and (3) ideographic writing systems usually use one character to represent one morpheme. The character itself may have parts that represent meaning and sound, such as Chinese characters in Chinese language.

Chinese characters are the written symbols of the Chinese language, and they make up one of the oldest writing systems in the world. The emergence and use of Chinese characters have had a major impact

不仅使汉语口语得以保留和传播，而且使中华文明得以传承和发展。汉字是中华民族进入文明社会的重要标志。汉字突破了时间的限制，后人可以通过汉字了解数千年来前人的思想、文化和成就；也可以通过汉字把当代的文化传给后代，使中华文明得以延续。汉字也突破了空间的限制，不仅在中国的不同方言区使用，也曾被周边国家和民族借用来记录不同的语言，而且流传到亚洲其他国家以及世界各国。不同国家和地区的人可以通过汉字或汉外翻译进行高效的交流。汉字不仅记录汉语口语，也独立于口语而存在，成为汉语书面语的书写形式，是人们进行思考和交流必不可少的工具。

1.2 汉字作为意音文字的主要特点

1. 汉字是世界上使用时间最长、使用人数最多的意音文字。虽然历史上出现过苏美尔人的楔形文字（图1-2）、古埃及的圣书字和中美洲的玛雅象形文字，但是这些原始文字早已停止使用。汉字的历史至少可以追溯到3500年以前，而且至今仍在广泛使用。除了中国以外，汉字也曾被越南、朝鲜、韩国、日本借去，用于记录他们的民族语言。今天，

on Chinese civilization, not only preserving and spreading the records of spoken Chinese, but also enabling Chinese civilization to be passed down and developed. Chinese characters are an important symbol of China's transition into a civilized society. Chinese characters have broken the limitations of time, allowing later generations to understand the thoughts, culture, and achievements of their predecessors over thousands of years. Through Chinese characters, culture can be passed on to future generations so that the Chinese civilization can continue. Chinese characters have also broken the limitations of space. They have not only been used in different dialect areas in China, but also by neighboring countries and nations to record different languages and have spread to other countries in Asia and around the world. People from different countries and regions can communicate effectively with Chinese characters and translation through the shared written language. Chinese characters not only record spoken Chinese, but they also exist independently of the spoken language. They are the written form of Chinese and are essential tools for people to think and communicate.

1.2 The Main Features of Chinese Characters as Ideographic Characters

1. Chinese characters are the ideographic writing system in the world; it is the longest-lasting writing language and boasts the largest

日本和韩国的文字系统中仍然使用一部分汉字；新加坡、马来西亚等国家也一定范围内使用汉字。汉字还是联合国正式使用的书写文字之一。

图 1-2　泥板上的楔形文字
Figure 1-2　Cuneiform writings on clay tablets

2. 汉字与汉语语素相对应。汉语书写的基本单位是字，这些字基本都是单音节的，汉语的语素也以单音节为主体。因此，用单音节的汉字来记录单音节的语素，两者基本吻合，一个字一个音节一个语素，一一对应，便于使用。中国古代诗歌一般分为五言诗和七言诗，五言诗每句五个字、五个音节、五个语素，七言诗则是每句七个字、七个音节、七个语素，形式整齐划一，语义上下对仗，读起来朗朗上口。但需要注意的是，语言的组成单位是词而不是字，古代汉语

number of users in the world. Although Sumerian cuneiform writings (Figure 1-2), Egyptian hieroglyphs, and Mayan hieroglyphs have appeared throughout history, these primitive writing systems have stopped being used. Chinese characters can be traced back to 3,500 years ago and are still widely used today. In addition to China's mainland, Chinese characters have also been borrowed by Vietnam, North Korea, South Korea and Japan to record their national languages. Today, some Chinese characters are still used in the writing systems of Japan and South Korea; Singapore, Malaysia and other countries also use Chinese characters to a certain extent. Chinese characters also act as one of the official writing systems used by the United Nations today.

2. Chinese characters correspond to Chinese morphemes. The basic unit of Chinese writing is a character. These characters are mostly monosyllabic. Chinese morphemes are mainly monosyllabic as well. Therefore, the monosyllabic Chinese characters are used to record the monosyllabic Chinese morphemes, creating a system in which one morpheme always represents a specific syllable. One character, one syllable, and one morpheme all correspond to each other, making Chinese characters easy to use. Ancient Chinese poetry generally is divided into five-character poems and seven-character poems. Five-character poems have five characters, representing five syllables and five morphemes, per line. Seven-character poems have seven characters,

的词汇多是单音节的，字和词相对应；而现代汉语词汇以双音节和多音节为主，因此，一个汉字不等于一个词。汉字是书写的单位，而词是语言的单位。单音节的汉字从形式上不能把词的界限显示出来，词和词之间也没有相隔的空间，以中文为第二语言的学习者在写作和阅读中需要格外留意。

3. 汉字是形音义的统一体。虽然汉字以表意为主，字形和字义联系紧密，但是大多数的字不但有形有义，而且还有音。很多汉字有意符，也有声符，在脱离上下文的情况下，一个单字的形体不仅有音有义，而且可以承载丰富的历史和文化因素。日本从 1995 年开始举办年度汉字评选活动，近些年来，亚洲不少国家也纷纷评选自己国家的年度字。年底的时候，举国上下，各行各业，男女老少，共同挑选一个最具代表性的年度汉字，用来概括这一年最显著的特点。比如，日本 2015 年的年度汉字是"安"，表达了这一年日本人对世界安全的担忧；中国 2016 年国内的年度字是"规"，国际的年度字是"变"，凸显了中国人对国内和国际形势的认识；马来西亚 2017 年的年度字是"路"，显示了对修路以及对

representing seven syllables and seven morphemes, per line. The poem's form is neat and uniform, the semantics are matching or antithetical between upper and lower lines, and the poems are often catchy. However, it should be noted that the constituent units of language are words rather than characters. The vocabulary of ancient Chinese is mostly monosyllabic, allowing words and characters to correspond; modern Chinese vocabulary, conversely, is dominated by two-syllable and multi-syllable words. Therefore, a Chinese character does not necessarily equal one word. Chinese characters are units of writing, but words are language units. Monosyllabic Chinese characters cannot display the boundaries of words. There is no space between individual words and words. Learners who use Chinese as a second language need to pay special attention to the characters while reading and writing.

3. Chinese characters are the unity of shape, sound and meaning. Chinese characters are mainly ideographic, meaning the glyphs and meanings are closely related. But most of the characters have shape, meaning and sound. Many Chinese characters have both meaning radicals and sound indicators. In the case of a single character, its shape not only shows the meaning and sound, but can also carry rich historical and cultural factors. In 1995, Japan began the practice of an annual Chinese character selection. In recent years, many Asian countries have also chosen to select an annual character. At

国家所走道路的关注。评选年度汉字这一活动恰恰反映了汉字的概括性、形象性、包容性等特点（图1-3）。

图 1-3   2022 年，中国一家媒体评选的
年度汉字是"韧"

Figure 1-3   In 2022, China's annual character selected by a Chinese media is "*Ren* (tenacity)".

4. 汉字具有超越时间的属性。在历史的长河中，中国发生了很多变化，但是古今汉字却保留了较强的一致性，无论是字形还是字义，在本质上基本是一致的，具有连续性。比如，两千多年前留下的《道德经》《论语》等经典文献，现代人仍然读得懂，仍然可以心领神会；唐诗宋词，仍然妇幼皆知，脍炙人口。中国数千年的历史和文化得以保留和传承是离不开汉字的。汉字起到了承前启后、使中国文化一脉相承的独特作用。反观同时代用拼音文字记录的文献，由于读音的变化，现代人已经很难读懂了。

5. 汉字具有超越地域的属性，因此成为不同方言（包括不同语言）共同的书写系统。汉语有不同的方言，十分复

the end of the year, all people in a country will select a most representative Chinese character together, using it to represent the most notable feature of the year. For example, Japan's 2015 annual character was "*An* (peace)", indicating the Japanese's concerns about world security that year; China's 2016 annual character domestically was "*Gui* (regulation)" and internationally was "*Bian* (change)", highlighting China's domestic and international perspectives; and Malaysia's 2017 annual character was "*Lu* (road)", which expressed concerns about building roads and the path their country was taking. The activity of selecting an annual Chinese character reflects the generality, image, and inclusiveness of Chinese characters (Figure 1-3).

4. Chinese characters have attributes that can cross time. In the long river of history, though many changes have taken place in China, ancient and modern Chinese characters have retained remarkably strong consistency. Both glyphs and their meanings are consistent in nature. For example, the classics such as *Tao Te Ching* and *The Analects*, which were written more than two thousand years ago, are still well understood by modern people and are well-received. Poetry in the Tang and Song dynasties is still known to common people in China, and is still very popular. China's thousands of years of history and culture cannot be preserved and passed down without Chinese characters. Chinese characters have played a special role in preserving the past and

杂，而且有些方言之间的语音差别很大，操不同方言的人往往无法交流。比如广东人说的广东话、福建人说的闽南话，北方人基本听不懂。但是，由于汉字具有"书同文"的特点，如果用汉字把他们的话写出来，大家就一目了然，沟通毫无障碍了（图1-4）。正是由于汉字特殊的表意功能，克服了拼音文字只能按一种语言或方言的发音来拼写的限制，因此无论说什么方言，由于基本的词汇和语法是一致的，用汉字写出来，都可以达到很好的交流目的。如果没有汉字，不同方言区的人就无法用口语交流，真是无法想象会出现什么情况。可以说，汉字为中国的长治久安和完整统一做出了重大贡献。日本、韩国之所以借用汉字来记录他们的语言，也是基于汉字的这一特点。

图1-4　汉字可以记录汉语不同的方言
Figure 1-4　Chinese characters can record different dialects of Chinese.

6. 汉字有助于大脑的平衡发展。美

shaping the future of Chinese culture. On the other hand, literature that uses the phonetic transcription can be difficult for modern people to understand due to the change of pronunciation.

5. Chinese characters can transcend regions and become a common writing system for different dialects and different languages. Chinese has different dialects, which are very complicated. Pronunciation of some dialects is also quite different, sometimes rendering communication between dialects impossible. For example, many northern Chinese people struggle to understand the Cantonese and Fujianese spoken by southern Chinese people. However, due to the regulation of the "unification of writing systems", if a southerner were to write their spoken words down using Chinese characters, northerners would immediately and precisely understand the southerners, effectively eliminating communication barriers (Figure 1-4). It is precisely because of the special ideographic function of Chinese characters that it overcomes the primary limitation of the phonetic text: it can only be spelled by the pronunciation of one language or dialect. Therefore, no matter which dialect is spoken, since Chinese characters' basic vocabulary and grammar are consistent, ideas can be written in Chinese characters, achieving successful communication. If there were no Chinese characters, people in different dialect areas could not communicate in spoken language, creating unimaginable consequences. It could

国神经心理学家斯佩里博士（1913—
1994）通过实验证实了大脑的"左右脑
分工理论"，并因此与其他两人共同荣
获1981年的诺贝尔生理学或医学奖。按
照这一理论，左脑负责语音，右脑主管
图形。由于拼音文字注重的是表音功能，
英语或其他印欧语的口语和拼写都由左
脑负责，左脑得到较多的刺激和训练，
所以有左脑强右脑弱的倾向。而书写汉
字时，不仅要考虑到字音，而且要涉及
字形，左脑管语音，右脑管文字，左右
脑并用，因而有助于大脑的平衡发展。

7. 从构形上说，汉字都是由笔画构
成的，笔画构成部首，部首再组合为单
字。部首的种类很多，而且具有不同的组
合方式（图1-5），所以每个汉字都有自
己独特的结构。此外，由于汉字与语素相
对应，语义是复杂的，汉字的数量自然也
很多。这些都给中国书法的发展提供了空
间，创造了条件。虽然汉字缺少完备的表
音系统，初学者看到汉字往往不知道如何
发音，但是这也增加了学习者的好奇心和
学习兴趣。

8. 汉字不仅是使用人数最多的文字
系统，而且也是世界上最具艺术性的书写
符号。艺术是人类创造力和想象力的表

be said that Chinese characters have made a significant contribution to China's long-term stability and unification. Japanese and Korean have borrowed Chinese characters to record their languages—further evidence that Chinese characters can cross the widest of space.

6. Chinese characters can facilitate balanced neurological development. American neuropsychologist, Dr. Roger Wolcott Sperry (1913–1994) and two colleagues were awarded the Nobel Prize in Physiology or Medicine in 1981 for their confirmation of the "left and right brain division theory". This occurred through various "split-brain research" experiments. According to this theory, the "left brain" is responsible for speech and the "right brain" is responsible for graphics. Because phonetic text focuses on the auditory function, the spoken and spelling of English or other Indo-European languages use the "left brain" almost exclusively. This gives the "left brain" more stimulation and training. This creates a tendency for the "left brain" to be strong and the "right brain" is weak. When writing Chinese characters, practitioners not only focus on the sounds, but also the glyphs. The "left brain" responds to speech while the "right brain" responds to text. This relatively equal stimulation of the "left" and "right" brains is conducive to achieving balanced neurological development.

7. Chinese characters are generally composed of strokes. Strokes form the radicals, and the radicals are combined into a

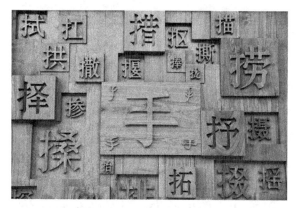

图 1-5　汉字"手"及由部首"扌"构成的其他字
Figure 1-5　Chinese character *Shou* and other characters composed of radical "*shou*".

达或应用，由此产生的作品主要因其美感或情感力量而受到赞赏。汉字的一笔一画都融入了中国人的审美观和创造性，反映了人们的观察能力和联想能力，体现了一种文化和精神。每个汉字的形体都是独立的、匀称的、有内涵的，既有形态美，又有立意美。每个汉字都像一幅美妙的抽象画，令人回味无穷。

随着中国和亚洲其他国家经济文化的发展，越来越多的人开始关注、学习和使用汉字。科技的发展也使汉字的处理越来越便利。汉字的输入、发音和翻译都可以利用电脑来操作。汉字作为世界文字系统中独具特色的重要成员，走向国际化已成为必然的发展趋势。

character. There are many types of radicals, and there are different combinations (Figure 1-5), so each Chinese character has its own unique structure. Moreover, since Chinese characters correspond to morphemes and semantics is complex, the number of Chinese characters is naturally large. These features have provided space for the development of Chinese calligraphy. Although due to the lack of a complete phonetic system in Chinese characters, beginners often do not know how to pronounce Chinese characters, it will make learners more curious and interesting to learn.

8. Chinese characters are not only the most used writing system in the world, but also the most artistic writing system. Art is the expression or application of human creativity and imagination that produce works to be appreciated primarily for their beauty or emotional power. Every Chinese character incorporates the aesthetics and the creativity of the Chinese people, reflecting their ability to observe and associate with the world, reflecting the culture and spirit. The shape of each Chinese character is independent, well-proportioned, and has an implicit meaning. Chinese characters have both beautiful form and artistic conception. Every Chinese character is like a beautiful abstract painting, which is both interesting and attractive.

More and more people are beginning to pay close attention to learning and using Chinese characters due to the economic and cultural development of China and other Asian countries. Scientific and technological development has made using Chinese characters more and more convenient, and computers can now be used for the input and translation of Chinese characters, as well as hearing their pronunciations. Because of their importance and uniqueness in terms of world writing systems, Chinese characters have inevitably become a significant international writing system.

思考题 Questions

1. 语言包括哪几个要素？文字是形成语言的要素之一吗？

2. 世界上大约有多少种语言？这些语言中有多少种语言有文字系统？

3. 口语和书面语有哪些不同？

4. 为什么说文字的产生是人类文明发展的里程碑？

5. 世界上的文字系统可以分为几种类型？每种文字类型的特点是什么？

6. 为什么说汉字是世界上使用人数最多、使用时间最长的文字？

7. 为什么日语、韩语等语言可以借用汉字作为它们的书写文字？

8. 你认为学习汉字可以帮助人们左右脑的平衡发展吗？为什么？

9. 什么是艺术？为什么说汉字是世界上最具艺术性的文字之一？

10. 你认为汉字跟你使用的书写系统有什么不同？

1. What are the elements that make up a language? Is a writing system one of the elements needed for the formation of a language?

2. How many languages are there in the world? How many of these languages have writing systems?

3. What is the difference between spoken language and written language?

4. Why is the emergence of a writing system considered as a major milestone in the development of human civilization?

5. How many types of writing systems can be divided in the world? What are the characteristics of each type of writing system?

6. Why are Chinese characters the most common and longest continuously used writing system in the world?

7. Why do Japanese, Korean, and other languages borrow Chinese characters for their writing systems?

8. Do you think that learning Chinese characters can help people's balance of left and right brain's development? Why?

9. What is art? Why are Chinese characters considered as one of the most artistic writing systems in the world?

10. What do you think is the difference between Chinese characters and the writing system you use?

第二章 汉字的起源、使用与自然美
Chapter Two The Origin, Use and Natural Beauty of Chinese Characters

2.1 汉字从哪里来?

中国的汉字是从什么时候开始使用的?汉字又是从哪里来的呢?这些问题直到 1899 年发现甲骨文以后才初步找到答案。当时任清朝(1616—1911)国子监祭酒的金石学者王懿荣(1845—1900)生病了,医生给他开的药方中有一味药叫"龙骨"。他十分惊奇地发现,从药店买回来的所谓"龙骨",上面竟然有很多刀刻的痕迹。他马上派家人到那家药店去买更多的"龙骨",结果发现这些"龙骨"上的刀痕可能就是一种古代文字。这些文字刻写于龟甲或兽骨之上,最初是从河南安阳小屯村出土的,而这里正是商朝后期(前 1300—前 1046)都城的遗址,当时称作"殷"。经过对照比较和猜测考证,他和其他精通古文字的学者终于从中药材"龙骨"中辨认出了甲骨文(图 2-1)。

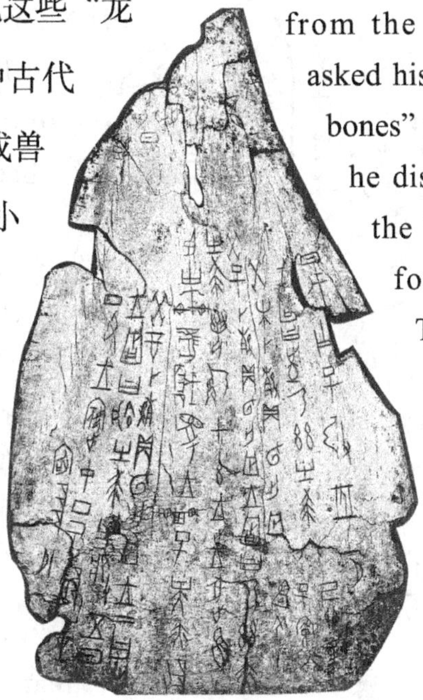

图 2-1 商代甲骨文
Figure 2-1 Inscriptions on a piece of tortoise shell, Shang Dynasty

2.1 Where Do Chinese Characters Come From?

When did the Chinese writing system begin to use? Where did Chinese characters come from? These questions were not initially answered until the discovery of oracle bone inscriptions in 1899. Mr. Wang Yirong (1845–1900), Minister of the Education Department of the Qing Dynasty (1616–1911), became sick. A Chinese medical doctor gave him a prescription in which one of the medicines was called "dragon bone". He found, with great surprise, that there were many knife markings on the "dragon bones" bought from the pharmacy. Immediately he asked his servants to buy more "dragon bones" from the pharmacy. As a result, he discovered that the markings on the "dragon bones" were ancient forms of Chinese characters. These characters were carved on tortoise shells or animal bones, unearthed from Xiaotun Village in Anyang County of Henan Province. This village was the site of the capital in the later period of Shang Dynasty (1300 B.C.–1046 B.C.) called "Yin". Through comparison and

从 1899 年至今，从殷墟发掘出的甲骨文刻片已超过 15 万片。这些用甲骨文书写而流传于世的文献涉及商代经济文化等方方面面的内容，其中以占卜的内容为主。这些甲骨片上的刻痕原本就是卜辞的记录。中国人的祖先将兽骨和龟甲放在火上烤，然后根据烧烤后产生的裂纹来预测将要发生的事，并直接记录在甲骨上，所以甲骨文也叫"卜辞"，即用作占卜的文字。由于这些文字是从殷墟发现的，所以也叫"殷墟文字"。到目前为止，已经辨认出来的甲骨文单字大约有 4500 个，而能够释读出来的有 2000 个左右。中国其他地方出土的青铜器皿上也发现了与甲骨文相似的原始文字。如果这些甲骨文是公元前 16 世纪到公元前 11 世纪的商代使用的，那么距今已有 3500 多年的历史了。那时的甲骨文形体结构相当复杂，已经是一种较为成熟的文字系统。不难想象，在甲骨文之前一定会有甲骨文的雏形或

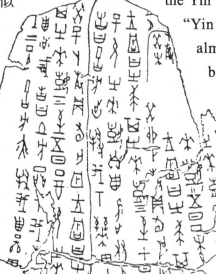

图 2-2　武丁时的卜辞
Figure 2-2　The divination during Wuding Period

textual research, he and other scholars who specialized in ancient Chinese scripts used the "dragon bones" to finally recognize the oracle bone inscriptions (Figure 2-1).

Over 150,000 pieces of tortoise shells with oracle bone inscriptions have been found from 1899 to the present. These inscriptions have provided a great deal of information on the economic and cultural situation during the Shang Dynasty. Their main focus is divination. These inscriptions were originally to record the divinations made by heating the animal bones and tortoise shells over a fire until cracks appeared. Predictions were read from the pattern of the cracks and written directly onto the animal bones or tortoise shells. Therefore, the oracle bone inscriptions are also known as "divination writings". Since these characters were discovered in the Yin ruins, they are sometimes called "Yin Ruins' Characters". There are almost 4,500 characters that have been recognized, 2,000 of which have been interpreted so far. Similar writings have been discovered on household utensils from other sites in China. If these oracle bone inscriptions were used from 1600 B.C. to 1100 B.C. during the Shang Dynasty, it indicates that the Chinese writing system has a history of over 3,500 years. The forms of the oracle bone inscriptions

其他形式的原始文字。因此可以肯定，中国的汉字产生于 3500 年以前，即在甲骨文出现之前。图 2-2 就是一个甲骨文刻片的例子。

根据考证，这个甲骨刻片上记录的大致内容是：

癸卯这一天进行占卜。卜官问："这一旬没有灾祸吧？"商王推断说："有灾祸，可能是外来的灾难吧？"到了七天以后的己巳，果然有来自西方的灾难。臣下报告说，敌方出动，侵袭我方，夺去七十田和五个人。[1]

甲骨文在汉字的形成与发展过程中起着承前启后的作用，而且中国汉字经历了从象形到抽象的复杂的转变演化过程。那么，最原始的中国汉字是由谁创造的呢？又是什么时候创造的呢？依照东汉（25—220）文字学家许慎（约 58—约 147，一说约 30—约 121）的说法，中国文字是仓颉独创的。据说，仓颉（图 2-3）是黄帝的史官，具有特殊的才能，甚至有人说他有四只眼睛。但文字是约定俗成的语言书写符号，是难以由一个人独立创造并被大众百姓普遍

at that time were quite sophisticated and the writings were mature. It is very reasonable to deduce that there was an embryonic form of oracle bone inscriptions or a primitive writing system. It is thus evident that Chinese characters were created more than 3,500 years ago, that is, before the oracle bone inscriptions appeared. Figure 2-2 is an example of oracle bone inscriptions:

According to the research, the basic message on this tortoise shell is as follows:

The divination was taken on the day of Guimao. The officer of divination asked if there would be a disaster within ten days. King of Shang inferred that there would be one, caused probably by the outsiders. As expected, the disaster came from the west side seven days later. An official reported that the enemy set out, and attacked us on the day of Jisi. They captured seventy pieces of land and five people.[1]

Oracle bone inscriptions play a connecting role in the formation and development of Chinese characters, and Chinese characters develop from pictograms to more abstract and sophisticated forms. So, who created the primitive form of Chinese characters and when? Based on Xu Shen (about 58–147/about 30–121), a famous philologist from the Eastern Han Dynasty, Chinese characters were created by Cang Jie (Figure 2-3), an official historian of Emperor Huang. It was said that Cang Jie had special

[1] 何九盈等（1995）《中国汉字文化大观》，北京：北京大学出版社。

[1] He, Jiuying et al. (1995) *Chinese Characters and Culture*. Beijing: Peking University Press.

接受的。荀子（前313—前238）说："好书者众矣，而仓颉独传者，壹也。"可以推断，远古时代有很多人创造出不同的文字，仓颉对这些文字进行搜集、整理、规范、统一，使之流传下来。这种说法看起来更有道理。汉字是由百姓大众所创造的，而仓颉起到了集中众人智慧的作用。传说仓颉生活在黄帝时代，距今大约4600多年。那么，汉字的起源应该在大约5000年以前，而甲骨文只是中国汉字使用了1000多年后形成的一种字体。

图 2-3　仓颉像
Figure 2-3　Statue of Cang Jie

　　自从中国人在社会生活的实践中创造了汉字，这一中文书写系统就成为记录与传播中国文化的主要媒介。正如我们从上面的甲骨文刻片和下面的毛公鼎（图2-4）中所看到的，在公元1000多年前，商代龟甲、兽骨和商周青铜器上这些最早的文字记录，无论是在形式上还是在内容上，都已经相当复杂。然而，迄今为止还没有发现比甲骨文更早的文字系统，只有从新石器时代的陶器（图2-5、图2-6）上找到的一些原始标记，

talents and that he even had four eyes. Since the characters are the writing symbols of a language established by popular usage, it is hard to believe that the characters could be created by a single person and accepted by the masses. Xunzi (313 B.C.–238 B.C.) said that, "There were many people specialized in writing, but Cang Jie was the one to put the characters together and hand them down." It can be inferred that many people created different characters in ancient times. These characters were collected, sorted out, standardized and unified by Cangjie to make them passed down. That seems more plausible. Chinese characters are created by the common people, and Cangjie plays the role of pooling the wisdom of the people. Legend has that Cang Jie lived in the period of Emperor Huang, which can be traced back to 4,600 years ago. Therefore, the primitive forms of the characters must have been created about 5,000 years ago. 1,000 years later, the oracle bone inscriptions developed based on these original forms.

The Chinese written language has served as the chief medium of recording and spreading Chinese culture since the creation of characters. As we can see from the oracle bone inscriptions above and Duke Mao Tripod (Figure 2-4) below, more than 1,000 years ago, the earliest written records on tortoise

图 2-4 西周时期的毛公鼎，铸有铭文 32 行、499 字，是现存青铜器中铭文最长的一篇，也是金文（钟鼎文）书法的典范

Figure 2-4 Duke Mao Tripod was cast in the Western Zhou Dynasty. 499 characters in 32 lines were inscribed on it. It is the extant bronze ware with the longest inscriptions and a classic example of calligraphy in bronze inscriptions.

这些可能就是汉字早期的雏形。

作为汉语的书写符号，中国汉字的字形由秦朝（前 221—前 206）的秦始皇（前 259—前 210）下令加以统一，实行标准化，并且一直使用到现在。虽然一些汉字中含有声符，但是汉字不是按字母组合的。由于中文的书写跟发音的准确与否没有直接关系，因此尽管口语已经发生了很大的变化，并形成了互有差别的许多地方方言，书面语却相对稳定。由于早期汉字是用来书写卜辞的，而且人们为了具备读写能力需要经过专门的学习

shells, animal bones and bronzes of the Shang Dynasty were quite complicated both in form and content. However, no writing system earlier than the oracle bone inscriptions has been discovered so far, only some primitive marks found on Neolithic pottery (Figure 2-5 & 2-6), which may be the embryonic forms of Chinese characters.

As the writing system of Chinese, the glyphs of Chinese characters were standardized by Emperor Qin Shihuang (259

图 2-5 西安半坡村的彩陶
Figure 2-5 Colored pottery excavated from the Banpo Village of Xi'an

图 2-6 半坡陶器上的刻画符号
Figure 2-6 Symbols on pottery excavated from the Banpo Village

和训练，所以中国人自然而然形成了对文字及相关学问的崇拜。在中国古代社会，莘莘学子为了走入仕途、光宗耀祖，必须熟知儒家经典著作并通过科举考试来实现自己的理想（图2-7）。这种历代相传的科班教育制度和对儒家经典的尊崇，使所有受过传统教育的中国人无论在何时何地都具有相似的文化背景和道德观念，并且给予书面语崇高的地位，甚至写有文字的纸都需要放到特殊的容器中焚烧后埋入地下或投入河流，不能随便处理（图2-8）。

B.C.–210 B.C.) of Qin Dynasty (221 B.C.–206 B.C.). They remain in use to the present day. Some of the characters contain phonetic elements, but the script is not alphabetic. Since literacy is not tied to the right pronunciation, the written language remains unaltered, whereas the spoken language has changed and become differentiated among many regional dialects. The early association of writing with divination and the difficulty of achieving literacy undoubtably contributed to the Chinese attitude of veneration for scholarship. In ancient Chinese society, successful candidates for public office achieved their positions of power and prestige

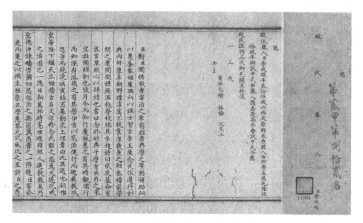

图 2-7　中国古代科举考试试卷
Figure 2-7　The test paper of the civil service examination in ancient China

图 2-8　"敬字亭"是专门用来焚烧字纸的
Figure 2-8　Jingzi Pavilion was specially used to burn paper with writing on it.

中国书面语到底有多少个汉字呢？大型字典中收录的汉字超过了10万个，清代的《康熙字典》（图2-9）收录了近5万个汉字。看起来数量惊人，但是其中多数的汉字很少使用。事实上，经常

by passing the civil service examinations based upon mastery of the Confucian classics (Figure 2-7). This common curriculum and the reverence for the Confucian classics united the educated Chinese across time and space and gave similar cultural background and moral values and gave greater status to the written

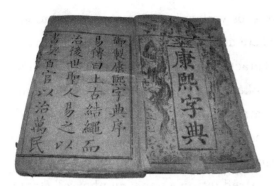

图 2-9　清代《康熙字典》
Figure 2-9　The *Kangxi Dictionary*, compiled in the Qing Dynasty

使用的汉字大约有 5000 个，而日常生活中常用的只有 3000 多个，这些汉字的使用率占日常书刊用字总数的 99%。在这 3000 多个常用汉字中，950 个汉字的使用频率最高，占书刊用字的 90%。因此，如果一个外国学生认识最常用的 1000 个汉字，那么基本上就可以阅读中文的日常读物了。从另一个角度看，大量的汉字以及各种各样独特的字形和笔画结构也给书法家提供了丰富的原材料。因此，中国书法比世界上任何其他语言的书法都要复杂得多。

此外，我们还应了解汉字的简化。由于汉字历史悠久，使用地域广阔，人口众多，用它记载的典籍数量多、时间跨度大，所以汉字体系总字数多、异体字多、一些字笔画数多（图 2-10），人们学习和使用起来有一定的困难。因此，人们开始简化汉字。汉字简化的主要途

system. Paper with writing on it needed to be burned in special receptacles, then buried underground or thrown into rivers, and can't be disposed casually (Figure 2-8).

How many characters are there in the Chinese written language? The large dictionary contains more than 100,000 characters. The *Kangxi Dictionary* (Figure 2-9) of the Qing Dynasty included nearly 50,000 characters. Although this may seem a great number of characters, many of those characters are seldom used. In fact, the frequently used characters are those that cover 99% of characters appearing in books and newspapers, a total of around 5,000, with only 3,000 or so used in everyday life. Among those 3,000 characters, 950 of them have the highest frequency of appearance, covering 90% of those printed in books and newspapers. Therefore, it is possible for a foreigner to be able to read in Chinese if he or she knows about 1,000 of the most frequently used characters. From another perspective, the large number of characters with their various forms and unique structure provide a large number of raw materials for the calligraphers. Chinese calligraphy is thus much more complicated than calligraphy in any other language.

In addition, we should also learn about the simplification of Chinese characters. Because of the long history of Chinese characters, the vast territory in which they were used, and the large population of people using them, the number of books and

图 2-10　一些 30 画的汉字
Figure 2-10　Some Chinese characters composed of 30 strokes

径是减省笔画。简化后的汉字称为"简体字"，相对而言，简化前的汉字称为"繁体字"。例如，"鸟"为简体字，"鳥"为繁体字。

　　在不同的历史时期，汉字都得到了不同程度的简化。简化后的汉字大大方便了人们的生活、学习和工作。目前，中国内地（大陆）按照 1986 年中国政府发布的修订后的《简化字总表》来推行简体字形，除特殊情况（如古籍出版、书法创作）外，就不再使用原有的繁体字形了。而中国香港、澳门和台湾等地区及海外部分地区目前仍使用繁体汉字。不过，在书法创作中，人们还是更多地使用繁体字形，以达到美观的效果。

　　可以说，汉字的产生与大自然的万事万物密不可分。汉字源于自然、融于自然，反映了自然之美——既安详静谧又生机勃勃，既运转规律又千变万化，

records written in Chinese continued to grow. There are many characters and many variant characters; some characters have too many strokes (Figure 2-10). As a result, Chinese characters became difficult to learn and to use. This led to the need to simplify Chinese characters. The main method of simplification is a reduction in the number of strokes. The set of post-simplification characters is known as "simplified characters". The set of pre-simplification Chinese characters is called "complex characters" or "traditional characters". For example, 鸟 is the simplified form and 鳥 is the complex form.

Simplified characters appeared in virtually every historical period. Simplified Chinese characters have brought great convenience to the lives, study and work of the Chinese people. Currently, the Chinese mainland follows a system of character standardization of the *Table of Simplified Chinese Characters* which was revised and reissued in 1986 by the Chinese government. For any character that was simplified, the traditional form can no longer be used except in special cases (such as the publication of ancient texts or calligraphic works). In China's Hong Kong, Macao, Taiwan, and other areas of the world, traditional characters are still in use. However, traditional characters are often used in calligraphic works to achieve the aesthetic effect.

It can be said that the production of Chinese characters is inseparable from all things in nature. Chinese characters

体现了和谐与动感的统一。汉字是人类想象力、审美观与大自然所呈现的千姿百态的完美结合。

2.2 汉字在东亚的使用

历史上，汉字曾经是亚洲很多国家的官方文字，越南、日本、朝鲜、韩国、新加坡、马来西亚等国都曾使用或借用过汉字。其中，朝鲜、日本、越南在历史上都曾将汉字作为正式的、唯一的书写系统。汉字之所以能够在东亚、东南亚等地区广泛使用，主要原因是汉字作为意音文字，具有表意的特点，可以用来记录不同的语言或方言。此外，汉字源于自然、融于自然，反映了自然之美。汉字发音动听，字体美观，表意清晰，让人们乐于使用，并在使用中得到美的享受。字义、字形、字音之美和大自然之美相融合，形成了汉字的书写之美。

朝鲜民族大致在公元元年前后引进汉字，早于其他东亚国家。公元 4 世纪，朝鲜设太学，汉字成为朝鲜官方规定的唯一的通用文字。直到 15 世纪中叶，李氏王朝第四代君主世宗才创制了朝鲜半岛最早的表音文字"训民正音"（即"谚文"）（图 2-11）。尽管如此，直到 19 世纪末，汉字仍占据正式文件的书写地位，

are derived from nature and blend in with nature, reflecting the beauty of nature—it is both serene and vigorous, with regularity of operation and ever-changing, reflecting the unity of harmony and movement. Chinese characters are the perfect combination of human imagination, aesthetics and the various poses presented by nature.

2.2 The Use of Chinese Characters in East Asia

Historically, Chinese characters used to be as the official writing system in many Asian countries. Vietnam, Japan, North Korea, South Korea, Singapore, Malaysia and other countries have used or borrowed Chinese characters. Among them, North Korea, Japan, and Vietnam historically used Chinese characters as their only official writing system. The main reason why Chinese characters are widely used in East Asia, Southeast Asia and other regions is that Chinese characters, as ideographic system, have ideographic characteristics. It can be used to record different languages or dialects. In addition, Chinese characters are derived from nature, blend in with nature, and reflect the beauty of nature. Chinese characters have beautiful sounds, fonts and clear meaning. People can enjoy the beauty while using Chinese characters. The beauty of the meaning, shape and sound of the characters and the beauty of nature are integrated to form the beauty of writing Chinese characters.

The Korean nation introduced Chinese

朝鲜的历史资料都是用汉字记录的。

图 2-11　朝鲜的《训民正音》
Figure 2-11　North Korea's *Xunmin Zhengyin*

据日本最早的历史文献《古事记》和《日本书纪》记载，汉字传入日本大约在 4 世纪或 5 世纪。有些研究结果显示的传入时代甚至更早。由于汉字从中国传入日本的时代和地区不同，音读上还有吴音、汉音和唐音之分。日本借用了汉字的读音和含义，并在汉字的基础上创造出了自己的本土文字——假名文字（图 2-12、图 2-13），但是在本民族文字体系中仍然保留着汉字。日文中有 2136 个标准汉字，日本小学生要学习 1006 个汉字。汉字已成为日本文化的一部分。比如，日本在每个时代都有流行的汉字，这些汉字反映了时代的特点和变化。日本人的姓也往往取自他们认为的意思较好的汉字，如"松、山、川"等表示自然之美的汉字。

characters into their written language around the first year of the Christian era, earlier than other East Asian countries. In the 4th century A.D., North Korea established Imperial College and set Chinese characters as the common writing system officially. This persisted until the middle of the 15th century. The Lee Dynasty's fourth generation monarch, Shi Zong, created the earliest phonogram of the Korean peninsula, *Xunmin Zhengyin* (i.e., Hangul) (Figure 2-11). However, until the end of the 19th century, Chinese characters still occupied the writing position of formal documents. The historical materials of North Korean are all recorded in Chinese characters.

According to Japan's earliest historical documents *Ancient Events* and *Japanese Books*, Chinese characters were introduced into Japan in about the 4th or 5th century. Some findings indicate earlier use. Due to the different times in which Chinese characters were introduced into Japan's different regions, different dialects and pronunciations emerged, such as pronunciations in *Wu*, *Han* and *Tang* dialects. Japan borrowed the pronunciation and meaning of Chinese characters, and created its own native characters on the basis of Chinese characters—kana characters (Figure 2-12 & 2-13). However, Chinese characters still remain in the national writing system. There are 2,136 standard Chinese characters in Japanese, and Japanese elementary school students are required to learn 1,006 Chinese characters. Chinese characters have become part of Japanese culture. For example, there

图 2-12 日本的平假名来源于汉字的草书
Figure 2-12 Japanese hiragana is derived from the grass style of Chinese characters.

图 2-13 日本的片假名来源于汉字的偏旁部首
Figure 2-13 Japanese katakana is derived from the radicals of Chinese characters.

古代越南人把汉字称为"儒字"，因为汉字是伴随着儒家《诗经》和《尚书》等经典著作传到越南的。968—1282 年，汉字是越南唯一的文字；13 世纪，"字喃"逐渐推广（图 2-14）；17 世纪，拼音化的国语字出现，但汉字仍是官方文字，占主导地位。越南许多重要的史书、公文都采用中国文言文。比如，研究越南早期历史最重要的史书之一《大越史记全书》就是由汉字文言文编撰而成的。

are certain popular Chinese characters in Japan in each era, and these Chinese characters reflect the characteristics and changes of the era. Japanese surnames are often taken from Chinese characters that they think have good meanings, such as pine, mountain, river, and other Chinese characters that express the beauty of nature.

The ancient Vietnamese called the Chinese characters "Confucian characters", since Chinese characters were introduced into Vietnam along with Confucian classics, such as *The Book of Songs* and *The Book of History*. In the year of 968–1282, Chinese characters functioned as the only written language of Vietnam. In the 13th century, chu nom was gradually popularized (Figure 2-14). In the 17th century, phonetic mandarin characters appeared, but Chinese characters remained the dominant official script. Many important history books and official documents were written in classical Chinese. For example, the *History of Greater Vietnam*, one of the most important historical books in Vietnam's early history, was compiled in classical Chinese.

Although Chinese characters influenced many Asian countries for a long time, Chinese characters were just the official writing language. It didn't correspond to the daily language used in various countries, so it was inconvenient to use. In modern times, countries began to emphasize national consciousness, and a movement to de-Chinese characters appeared in the "East Asian Chinese Character Circle". The highest degree of de-

图 2-14　越南的字喃
Figure 2-14　Vietnamese chu nom

　　虽然汉字在很长一段时间内影响了亚洲多个国家，但汉字毕竟只是官方文字，跟各国的日常语言不对应，使用起来不太方便。到了近代，各国开始强调民族意识，于是东亚汉字圈内出现了"去汉字化"运动。去汉字化程度最高的应该是越南。1945 年，越南独立后废除汉字，取而代之的是 17 世纪传教士发明的使用罗马字转写的"国语字"。现在的越南文字已经看不出汉字的痕迹了。在朝鲜半岛，二战之后，朝鲜废除汉字，以谚文作为国语；韩国也规定公文必须用谚文书写，并全面停止汉文教育。

　　相比之下，日本对于汉字的接受程度更高，并把中国汉字逐渐演变为日本汉字。1200 年前，日本人就开始用简化的汉字创造了音节字母；800 多年前，这套字母体系渐趋成熟。现行的 2136 个日本汉字中，有 300 多个进行了简化。在汉字研究上颇有建树的笹原宏之先生认为，汉字虽然在日本发生了很大的变化，

Chinese characters took place in Vietnam. In 1945, after Vietnam gained independence, Chinese characters were abolished. They were replaced with "national language characters", written in Roman letters, invented by missionaries of the 17th century. Now, the Vietnamese text contains no traces of Chinese characters. In the Korean peninsula, after the World War II, Chinese characters were abolished and Hangul was adopted as the national language. South Korea has also made it mandatory for official documents to be written in Hangul and stopped teaching Chinese altogether.

In contrast, Chinese characters in Japan seem to be acceptable. Japanese gradually evolved Chinese characters into Japanese characters. Japanese began to use simplified Chinese characters to create syllables about 1,200 years ago, and this alphabet system gradually matured 800 years ago. There are currently 2,136 Japanese characters, of which more than 300 have been simplified. Mr. Hiroyuki Sasahara, who has made great achievements in the study of Chinese characters, believes that although Chinese characters have undergone great changes in Japan, those changes show the flexibility, diversity and evolution of Chinese characters.

In the history of modern China, some scholars also think that Chinese characters should be reformed and should be moved towards Romanization. However, in the process of the changes and evolution of Chinese characters in recent years, the

但是这些变化显示了汉字的灵活性、多样性和演进的可能性。

在近代中国历史上，也有一些学者认为汉字应该改革，应该走上世界共同的拼音化方向。但是，在近些年汉字变化和演进的过程中，"汉字文化圈"国家发现"去汉字化"这条路越走越艰难，因为去掉汉字不但会破坏他们整个的语音系统，而且更是一种人为割裂历史的行为。就朝鲜半岛而言，由于汉字使用了近 2000 年，要将古代官方文件、历史著作、文学作品中的汉字完全抹去，那历史文献就所剩无几了。韩语中约有70% 的词汇来自汉语，同音异义的词也很多，因此作为表音文字的韩文没有汉字就容易出现歧义。汉字在日本的改良虽然比较温和，但也造成了一定的混乱：原有的汉字词使用假名书写，出现了大量冗长的假名，导致很多人不会读这些日本汉字。

近年来，汉字逐渐在那些退出汉字圈的国家中复兴。一些学者指出，汉字不仅仅是中国的文字，也是东亚的国际文字，能使不同语言的民族以文字互相沟通；同时，汉字又与表音文字相容并存，能大大促进东亚各国间的交流合作。

countries in "Chinese Character Cultural Circle" have found that the "de-Chinese characters" is getting harder and harder to achieve. Removing Chinese characters not only destroyed their entire phonetic system, but also artificially cut off history. As far as the Korean peninsula is concerned, North and South Korea have collectively used nearly 2,000 years of Chinese characters. If they want to completely erase the Chinese characters in ancient official documents, historical works, and literary works, little to none of this history will be left. About 70% of Korean language come from Chinese language and the Korean language also contains many homophones. As a phonogram, the Korean writing system without Chinese characters is easily prone to ambiguity. Although the reform of Chinese characters in Japan was milder, it also caused some confusion. When the original Chinese characters were written in kana, resulting in a large amount of lengthy kana, many Japanese people could not read such writing.

In recent years, the revival of Chinese characters gradually emerged among those nations who quit. Some scholars have pointed that Chinese characters are not only the writing system of China, but also the international characters of East Asia. These universally understood characters enable people of different languages to communicate with each other in writing, while retaining their own phonograms, thus promoting exchanges and cooperation among East Asian countries.

思考题 Questions

1. 中国早期的文字是什么时候在什么地方发现的?

2. 清代学者王懿荣从"龙骨"上发现了什么?

3. 甲骨文主要记述的是什么?

4. 在发掘出的甲骨刻片上的汉字中,有多少已被辨认出来?又有多少能被释读出来?

5. 许慎是谁?你同意"汉字是由仓颉创造的"这一观点吗?

6. 早期汉字是什么时候进行第一次规范的?

7. 大型字典中共收录了多少个汉字?在日常生活中使用频率较高的汉字有多少个?中文学习者需要学习多少个使用频率最高的汉字?

8. 为什么说"汉字源于自然、融于自然,反映了自然之美"?

9. 历史上,汉字在哪些亚洲国家曾作为正式的书写系统?如果这些国家不再使用汉字,会产生什么问题?

10. 为什么汉字作为世界上最古老的书写文字能够使用至今,而且在现代依然能够复兴?

1. When and where were ancient Chinese characters discovered?

2. What did Mr. Wang Yirong of the Qing Dynasty find on the "dragon bones"?

3. What was the main focus of the oracle bone inscriptions?

4. How many Chinese characters have been recognized on the unearthed tortoise shells? How many can be interpreted?

5. Who was Xu Shen? Do you agree that the characters were created by Cang Jie?

6. When were the earliest Chinese characters first standardized?

7. How many characters are contained in the large Chinese dictionary? How many of them are the frequently used characters in daily life? How many characters with the highest frequency of appearance should a Chinese learner know?

8. Why is it said that "Chinese characters are derived from nature, blend in with nature, and reflect the beauty of nature"?

9. In which Asian countries have Chinese characters been historically used as the official writing system? What will happen if these countries stop using Chinese characters?

10. As one of the oldest written systems in the world, why Chinese characters can be used until today and can still be revived in modern times?

第三章　汉字的"六书"与寓意美
Chapter Three　The "Six Categories" and Beautiful Implication of Chinese Characters

可以说，所有文字都是从图画开始的，但是图画并不等于文字。如唐兰先生所说，"真正的文字，要到象意文字发生才算成功的"，当一般人"希望把复杂的事物用图画的方式记录下来时，文字就发生了"[1]。汉字的创造和发展也是这样一个渐进的过程。

根据古老的传说，中国文字的发明者叫仓颉。他从观察飞禽走兽在沙滩上或其他物体上留下的爪痕足印中得到启示，然后从那些能代表不同事物的图形中构想出简单的符号，比如下面的一些例子（图 3-1）：

It could be said that all of the writing systems started from pictures. However, pictures are not equivalent to the writing system of languages. As Mr. Tang Lan said, "The written language is not formed until the pictographic script was established". "The script appeared when people had the desire to record complicated things in the form of pictures."[1] This was the same procedure by which Chinese characters were created and developed.

According to an ancient legend, Cang Jie, the inventor of Chinese writing, got his ideas from observing natural phenomena such as animals' footprints and birds' claw marks on sand or other objects. He then worked out simple images of different objects such as the examples below (Figure 3-1):

图 3-1　Figure　3-1

---

[1] 唐兰（1979）《中国文字学》，上海：上海古籍出版社。

[1] Tang, Lan (1979) *The Chinese Philology*. Shanghai: Shanghai Classics Publishing House.

事实上，没有人能够创造出一种书写系统为所有使用这种语言的人所接受。中文书写系统是长期以来约定俗成的结果。中国文字学家许慎在《说文解字》一书中提出了"六书"的学说，他认为中国汉字是通过六种造字法而产生的。"六书"学说清楚地揭示了汉字的来源，同时也为人们解释每个汉字的意思和读音提供了很好的线索。《说文解字》把汉字分为"文"和"字"，"文"指独体字，而"字"表示合体字。"说文"就是解说独体字，"解字"则是分析合体字。对于外国学生来说，了解汉字的来源，不仅可以帮助记忆汉字，而且可以增加学习的兴趣。同时，通过书法练习，学生也会进一步掌握汉字的结构，了解汉字与大自然之间美的联系。

下面分别介绍六种造字法。

3.1 象形字

远古的中国汉字来源于图画，当时造字最主要的方法就是用图画来代表想要表达的事物。但是，越想逼真地表示某个事物，图形就会越复杂，花费的时间也就越多。因此，随着文字运用得越来越广，人们自然而然地倾向于用简

In fact, no person could possibly create a writing system that would be accepted by everyone who used the language. The Chinese writing system was established by popular usage and accepted by common practice over a long period of time. In his book *Shuowen Jiezi*, the Chinese philologist Xu Shen proposed *Liushu* theory. He believed that Chinese characters were produced through the six categories of writing. The *Liushu* theory clearly reveals the origins of Chinese characters and provides good clues as to the meaning and pronunciation of each character. In the book of *Shuowen Jiezi*, Xu Shen divides all characters into *wen* and *zi*. The section of *wen* covers the single characters while *zi* refers to the compound characters. *Shuowen* means to explain the single characters and *Jiezi* is to analyze the compound ones. For foreign students, understanding the origins of Chinese characters not only makes it easier to memorize the characters, but it also makes the learning more interesting. At the same time, through practice of calligraphy, students can also further understand the structure of each character and the connection between the beauty of characters and of nature.

The six categories are explained in the following section.

3.1 Pictographic Characters

Ancient Chinese characters were derived from pictures. The main method of creating characters at that time was to use pictures to represent what one wanted to express.

单的线条粗略勾勒出事物的形状。比如说，远古的中国人用"Ꭲ"的图形来表示"人"，用"�門"来表示"门"。这些字实际上是那些在远古时代单纯代表具体事物的抽象化的图形。象形字多为独体字。

由于象形字的来源是图画，而人们生活中的很多活动，尤其是抽象的思维概念难以用图画来表示，能画出来的具体的东西总是有限的，所以真正的象形字在汉字中所占的比例也是有限的。根据清代文字学家朱骏声（1788—1858）《说文通训定声·六书爻列》的统计，象形字共364个，大约占当时汉字总字数的3.9%（《说文解字》共收录9353个汉字）。随着文字的发展，象形字逐步简化，象征性增强，人们也逐渐放弃了这种造字的方法。但是，把象形字作为基本义符，用它造出新的合体字则是十分常见的，所以掌握基本的象形字是非常重要的。

However, the more detailed and true to life the graph is, the more complicated and time-consuming it is to create. Therefore, as the writing became more widely used, people naturally tended to outline the rough shape of the character with simple lines. For example, ancient Chinese people used "Ꭲ" to symbolize "*Ren* (person)", and used "�門" to mean "*Men* (door)". These characters were actually the symbolized pictures in ancient times, most of which were single characters.

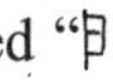

Pictographic characters took their origins from pictures. However, there were many activities in ancient times that included abstract concepts and could not be easily represented in the pictorial forms. The concrete things that can be drawn were always limited, so the proportion of real pictographic characters in Chinese characters was also limited. The pictographic characters totalling 364 only possess a small percentage of the Chinese characters, approximately 3.9% according to the statistics in *Shuo Wen Tong Xun Ding Sheng · Liushu Yaolie*, a book written by Zhu Junsheng (1788–1858), a philologist of the Qing Dynasty. There are 9,353 Chinese characters in *Shuowen Jiezi*. As the writing system matured, the pictographic characters gradually became simplified and symbolic. People have gradually given up this method to create new characters. However, it is very common to use a pictographic character as a "meaning element" in the creation of compound characters. Thus, it is important to master the basic pictographic

◈ 你能不能找出与下列早期象形字相对应的现代汉字及它们的英文意思，并用线连起来呢？

◈ Can you match the following ancient pictographic characters with their modern versions and English meanings?

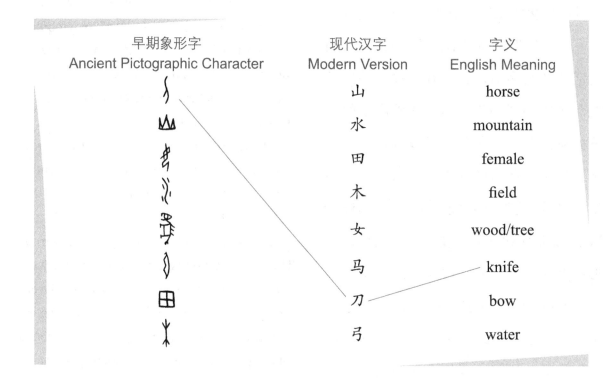

从上面的练习中，你能看出早期的象形字和它们的现代字形有哪些差异吗？总的来说：

（1）早期象形字的笔画比较弯曲，而现代汉字的笔画则比较平直。

（2）现代象形字的字形是方块形，更具有象征性，不再刻意模仿事物的原型。

characters.

From the above exercises, what are the differences between the ancient pictographic characters and their modern versions? Generally speaking:

(1) The curving strokes of the ancient pictographic characters have changed to flat, straight strokes of modern characters.

(2) The modern characters are no longer imitations of things they refer to, but are square and more symbolic in form.

3.2 指事字

这种造字法是通过特殊的符号来指明汉字所要表达的意思。众所周知，许多事物难以用绘图来表示清楚，因为它们的意思比较抽象，或者只是一个东西的某一部分。那么古代中国人是怎样创造汉字来表达这些事物的呢？

事实证明，他们采用抽象的符号来指明所要表示的意思。这样的符号完全是象征性的。比如，在一个较长的横线下方画一条短线构成"⌒"，以此来表明"在下面"的意思。还有一类指事字是通过在象形字上添加笔画来表达抽象的意义。比如，在表示"火"的象形字的上方加一条短线，就形成了一个新的汉字"灭"，表示把火灭掉的意思。随着时间的推移，这个汉字的意思得到引申和扩展，又有了"消亡"或"不存在"等意思，如"灭亡"或"灭绝"。指事字往往用来表明具体事物的某一点，多为独体字，在汉字中所占的比例较小。根据朱骏声《六书爻列》的统计，指事字共125个，只占约1.3%，而且很早以前就不再采用这种方法造字了。

3.2 Indicative Characters

This method of character creation indicates the meaning of Chinese characters through special symbols. As we all know, many things cannot be drawn out in pictures, for they may be abstract in meaning or just part of something. So how did the ancient Chinese create characters to express these things?

As it turned out, they used abstract symbols to indicate meanings. These symbols are purely symbolic. For example, positioning a short line under a longer one "⌒" indicates the meaning of "below". Another type of indicative characters is to add a stroke(s) to a pictographic character to express an abstract meaning(s). For instance, when a short line is put on the top of "火 (*Huo*)", it forms a new character "灭 (*Mie*)", which means "to put out a fire". As the time passed, this character gained new meanings, such as "to die out" or "to completely lose". Indicative characters usually represent one part of a physical object, most of which are single characters and account for a small proportion in Chinese characters. According to the statistics in Zhu Junsheng's *Liushu Yaolie*, indicative characters represent 125 characters (or 1.3%) of all characters. This method to create new characters was discontinued early on in Chinese history.

◆ 请把与下列早期指事字相对应的现代汉字及它们的英文意思用线连起来。

◆ Please match the ancient indicative characters listed below with their modern versions and English meanings.

早期指事字 Ancient Indicative Character	现代汉字 Modern Version	字义 English Meaning
	上	sky
	刃	fork
	本	*a unit for measuring length*
	末	excessively
	旦	end
	寸	root
	天	above
	太	dawn
	叉	blade

3.3 会意字

会意字是把两个或两个以上的义素组合在一起而形成的汉字。当远古的中国人必须表达一个复杂的概念，且这个概念不能用一个单一的图形来表示时，他们便把两个或两个以上的象形字合并使用，用它们组合的意思来描述一个行为或概念。会意字大部分为合体字，在汉字中所占比例高于象形字和指事字。根据朱骏声的统计，会意字共 1167 个，大约占 12.5%。这种造字法直到今天都还

3.3 Suggestive Characters

Suggestive characters are Chinese characters formed by combining two or more sememes. When the ancient Chinese had to express a complicated concept that could not be represented by a single picture, they tried to put two or more pictographic characters side by side to describe an action or a concept. Most of the suggestive characters are the compound characters, which account for a higher proportion than pictographic and indicative characters. According to Zhu Junsheng's statistics, suggestive characters represent a total of 1,167 characters (or approximately 12.5%) of all characters.

在使用。

举例来说，如果想表示光亮，就把表示太阳的 "日"（☉）和表示月亮的 "月"（☽）组合到一起，组成 "明"（◎☽）字。如果把 "人"（𠆢）字和表示树的 "木"（𣎳）字放在一起，形成 "休"（𠇋）字，即一个人靠在树干上，自然就合成了 "休息" 的意思。

People still continue to create new characters by this method today.

For example, the character "明 (*Ming*, bright)" is made by putting "日 (*Ri*, sun)" and "月 (*Yue*, moon)" together to express the concept of brightness. If the characters "人 (*Ren*, person)" and "木 (*Mu*, wood/tree)" representing the tree are put together to form the character "休 (*Xiu*, to rest)". That is, a person leans against the tree trunk, which naturally conveys the concept of rest.

◈ 请把与下列早期会意字相对应的现代汉字及它们的英文意思用线连起来。

◈ Please match the ancient suggestive characters listed below with their modern versions and English meanings.

早期会意字 Ancient Suggestive Character	现代汉字 Modern Version	字义 English Meaning
	好	space
	雷	good
	森	to follow
	分	to divide
	从	thunder
	男	country/kingdom
	间	forest
	国	male

3.4 形声字

形声字一般包括两个部件，即表义的形符和表音的声符。形符表示一个形声字所属的意义范畴，声符标示该字的

3.4 Pictophonetic Characters

Two elements, a pictorial and a phonetic radical, are put together to form a pictophonetic character. The pictorial radical indicates the general meaning to which the character

发音。尽管中国文字不属于表音文字系统，但是绝大部分汉字都具有这两个要素——一个表示声音的声旁和一个表示意义的形旁。事实上，文字的数量越多，形声字所占的比例就越大。根据朱骏声的统计，形声字有 7697 个，约占 82.2%。

举例来说，"妈"（mā）字的形旁"女"表示意义，声旁"马"（mǎ）标示相联系的字音。由于发音的变化，很多声旁已不能标示出带有该声旁的形声字的准确发音，只有少量的声旁带有标音的作用。但是这些声旁对于模拟汉朝时期的汉字发音仍很有价值。据唐兰先生统计，声旁的数目在 1000 个以上。[1] 由于每个形声字都带有音和义两方面的信息，因此对记忆和理解都很有帮助，特别是如果能记住并掌握一些最常用的偏旁。

belongs; the phonetic radical indicates the pronunciation of the character. Even though Chinese characters do not belong to a phonetic writing system, most of the characters consist of these two elements—a pictorial radical to represent the meaning and a phonetic radical for the pronunciation. In fact, the more characters available, the more pictophonetic characters can be produced. According to Zhu Junsheng's statistics, there are 7,697 (or about 82.2%) pictophonetic characters of all characters.

For instance, the character "妈 (mother)", pronounced as "*mā*": the pictorial radical "女 (female)" carries the meaning and the phonetic radical "马 (horse)" indicates the pronunciation. Due to the change of pronunciation over time, many phonetic radicals can not indicate the accurate pronunciation of a pictophonetic character with the phonetic radical, only a few still do. However, it is still valuable to have these phonetic radicals as they can provide clues as to the pronunciation simulation of the Chinese characters during the Han Dynasty. According to Mr. Tang Lan's statistics, there are over 1,000 phonetic radicals in the Chinese writing system.[1] Since the two elements of a pictophonetic character represent sound and meaning, it is helpful for memorization and understanding of characters if you can master some of the most commonly used ones.

---

[1] 唐兰（1979）《中国文字学》，上海：上海古籍出版社。

---

[1] Tang, Lan (1979) *The Chinese Philology*. Shanghai: Shanghai Classics Publishing House.

◈ 请参考下列形声字的字义和例字，分别写出每个形声字的声旁和形旁。

◈ Please refer to the meanings and examples of the following pictophonetic characters, and write the phonetic radical and pictorial radical of each character separately.

发音 Pronunciation	汉字 Character	声旁 Phonetic Radical	形旁 Pictorial Radical	形旁的意思 Pictorial Meaning	字义 English Meaning
jī	机	几	木	wood/tree	machine
huǒ	伙			person	partner
xiǎng	想			heart	to want
hé	河			water	river
qiǎng	抢			hand	to rob
nǎi	奶			female	grandmother
zhōng	钟			metal	clock
cài	菜			grass	vegetable
è	饿			food	hungry

3.5 假借字

假借字是借用读音相同或相近的字来表示一个完全不同的意思。借用的是字形和字音，表达的却是另外一个概念，所以一个字代表着两个概念。举例来说，"来"字原来表示"小麦"的意思，而当时难以通过象形的方法表示"到达"或"出现"的意思，于是就借用了同音字或近音字"来"（小麦）表达"到来"。慢慢地，"来"字的本义"小麦"丢失了，而借来的意思却得到了广泛使用。罗杰

3.5 Borrowed Characters

Borrowed characters are characters that borrow the same or similar sounds to express different meanings. The new character borrows the graph and pronunciation of a character, but represents a different concept. As a result, one character represents two concepts. For instance, *Lai* originally meant "wheat". Since it was hard to represent "arrive" or "appear" relying on pictographic or other devices, the character "*Lai* (wheat)" was borrowed to represent those concepts due to the similar sounds of the two characters. Gradually, the original meaning of "*Lai*

瑞指出，由于语法成分难以用象形的方法表示，所以早期这样的字基本上都是采用假借的方法来造字的。[1]根据朱骏声的统计，假借字共 115 个，大约占 1.2%。

3.6 转注字

最后一个种类叫转注，即某些字虽然发音有些差别，但有相同的部首或近似的字义，从而被当作另一个字使用。如"老"和"考"，都有相同的部首"耂"，而且都有"时间长"的意思，但是发音不同。这类字所占比例极小，只有 7 个，大约只占 0.07%，而且如何划分存在争议。

表 3-1 列出了朱骏声统计的"六书"的字数和占比：

表 3-1

六书	字数	占比
象形	364	3.84%
指事	125	1.32%
会意	1167	12.32%
形声	7697	81.23%
假借	115	1.21%
转注	7	0.07%

(wheat)" faded out and the borrowed meaning of "*Lai* (to come)" became widely used. Jerry Norman points out, "Grammatical elements were particularly hard to represent in pictorial form; as a result, virtually all the early graphs for such elements are based on this 'phonetic borrowing' principle."[1] According to Zhu Junsheng's statistics, borrowed characters represent a total of 115 characters (or about 1.2%) of the total characters.

3.6 Etymological Characters

The last category contains characters that have identical radicals or somewhat similar meanings, but with different pronunciations. Therefore, it is used as another character. For example, "老 (*Lao*)" and "考 (*Kao*)" share the same radical "耂", and both have the meaning of "a long time", but they have different pronunciations. Only 7 characters (approximately 0.07%) belong to this category, with the distinction of this category being debated among the scholars for a long time.

Table 3-1 lists the number and proportion of the "six categories" according to Zhu Junsheng:

Table 3-1

Six Categories	Number	Proportion
Pictographic Characters	364	3.84%

[1] 罗杰瑞（1995）《汉语概说》，北京：语文出版社。

[1] Norman, Jerry (1995) *Chinese*. Beijing: Language & Culture Press.

注：朱骏声在《说文解字》的基础上将统计的字数增加到9475个，表中每类字的百分比都是依此计算的。

在这六种造字方法中，许多学者认为假借和转注不应该列入造字法，它们实际上是活用汉字的方法，只有前四类（即"四书"）直接关系到汉字的结构。

人们普遍认为，汉字是象形文字，每个汉字都是一幅画儿。其实，虽然有些汉字的确是从图画发展而来的，但是这些汉字只占一小部分。绝大多数汉字是形声字，包括声符和义符。声符标示汉字原来的读音，尽管这些读音现在可能已经发生了很大的改变。

"六书"总结归纳了汉字的造字法和用字法，为我们提供了解析汉字和追根溯源的途径，也为学习汉字提供了线索和窍门。通过观察也可以看到，运用汉字"六书"所造的字，个个都真实自然，生动形象，寓意丰富。人们通过创造汉字来反映自己对事物的认识，每个汉字都是传达信息、交流情感的书面符号。我们可以通过对字形字义的分析，去领悟造字者所要传达的信息，并感受到汉字的寓意之美。每个汉字都可以让人如见其形，如闻其声，如感其意，既是表意的符号，又是视觉的享受。（图3-2）

Continued Table

Six Categories	Number	Proportion
Indicative Characters	125	1.32%
Suggestive Characters	1167	12.32%
Pictophonetic Characters	7697	81.23%
Borrowed Characters	115	1.21%
Etymological Characters	7	0.07%

Note: Zhu Junsheng increased the number of characters counted to 9,475 on the basis of *Shuowen Jiezi*, and the percentage of each type of character in the table was calculated according to this.

In these six categories, many scholars argue that categories (5) and (6) should not be considered as ways to create characters. Instead these categories indicate the different ways of how to use characters. They argue that only the first four categories (*Sishu*) are directly related to the composition of characters.

It is universally accepted that Chinese characters are pictographic and that each Chinese character represents a picture. It is true that some Chinese characters have developed from pictures, but they only comprise a small portion of the characters. The vast majority of Chinese characters are pictophonetic characters consisting of a phonetic radical and meaning radical. The phonetic radical indicates its original pronunciation which may, or may not,

图 3-2　汉字"福"的各种创意变形设计
　　　　带给人视觉的享受

Figure 3-2　Various creative deformation designs of the Chinese character "*Fu* (blessing)" bring people visual enjoyment.

represent its present pronunciation.

The "six categories" of Chinese characters summarized the methods of creating Chinese characters and flexibly using them, providing us with a way to analyze Chinese characters and trace their roots, as well as clues and tricks for learning Chinese characters. Through observation, we can also see that the characters created by using the six categories are all true and natural, vivid and rich in meaning. People reflect their knowledge of things by creating Chinese characters. Each Chinese character is a written symbol that conveys information and communicates emotion. We can comprehend the information conveyed by the creators through the analysis of the shape and meaning of the characters, and feel the beauty of meaning. Each Chinese character can be seen in its original form, sound and meaning after its creation. It is both an ideographic symbol and a visual enjoyment (Figure 3-2).

思考题 Questions

1. 所有的文字系统都起源于图画吗？

2. "六书"学说有什么意义？请列出许慎提出的"六书"的内容。

3. "象形字"来源于什么？象形字在汉字中所占比例是多大？为什么？

4. "指事字"有什么特点？请举例说明怎样用这种方法造字。

5. 什么是"会意字"？为什么古代中国人要用这种方法造字？

6. "形声字"包括几个部件？每个部件的功用是什么？形声字在汉字总数中所占比例是多大？

7. 什么是"假借字"？

8. 什么是"转注字"？

9. "六书"对学习汉字有什么帮助？

10. 你是否同意每个汉字"既是表意的符号，又是视觉的享受"？为什么？

1. Did all of the world's writing systems derive from pictures?

2. What was the significance of the *Liushu* theory? List the "six categories" proposed by Xu Shen.

3. What is the origin of pictographic characters? What percentage of Chinese characters are pictographic and why?

4. What are the characteristics of indicative characters? Please give examples to show how to create this type of characters.

5. What are the suggestive characters? Why did ancient Chinese people have to create this type of characters?

6. How many elements are there to form a pictophonetic character and what is the function of each element? What is the percentage of total characters that belongs to this category?

7. What are the borrowed characters?

8. What are the etymological characters?

9. How do the "six categories" of Chinese character creation help in learning Chinese characters?

10. Do you agree that each Chinese character "is both an ideographic symbol and a visual enjoyment"? Why?

第四章　汉字笔画、笔顺的线条艺术

Chapter Four　The Line Art of Chinese Characters' Strokes and Stroke Order

4.1 汉字的笔画

1. 什么是笔画

笔画是构成汉字字形的最小连笔单位。无论中文还是日文、韩文，在书写正体汉字的时候都要从笔画开始。汉字笔画是一套由点和线组成的系统，通过不同的组合构成不同的汉字。每一次从落笔到起笔所写出的点或线就叫作一笔或一画，因而也包括改变了方向的连笔单位。每个汉字都是由不同的笔画构成的。最简单的汉字只有一个笔画，而最复杂的可以多达五六十笔（图 4-1）。

图 4-1　biáng 字一共有 56 画
Figure 4-1　Character *Biang* has 56 strokes in total.

汉字的笔画是历史形成的。古文字没有笔画的概念。篆书笔形圆转，很难分出落笔和起笔的位置；从隶书开始，逐渐形

4.1 The Strokes of Chinese Characters

1. What is a stroke

A stroke is the smallest unit to form a character. Whether these written characters originate from the Chinese, Japanese or Korean languages, all of them begin with strokes. The stroke of Chinese characters is a system composed of dots and lines, which may be arranged and combined to form different Chinese characters. One single stroke includes all the motions necessary to produce a given part of a character before lifting the writing instrument from the writing surface; thus, a single stroke may also include changes in direction within the line without interruption. Each character is composed of different strokes. The simplest character consists of only one stroke in contrast to the most complex with fifty to sixty strokes (Figure 4-1).

The stroke of Chinese characters gradually was formed over the course of the language history. No concept of stroke exists in ancient Chinese script. It is difficult to distinguish individual strokes between the starting and ending points in ancient seal script. The straight strokes gradually were formed via clerical script. However, it was not until the emergence of regular script that the stroke rules and system of Chinese characters

成了平直的笔画。不过，直到楷书出现才逐步确定了汉字的笔画规则和系统。

2. 笔画的作用

了解汉字的笔画和笔画组合模式对于学习汉字和书法是十分重要的。首先，无论学习汉字的笔画顺序还是汉字的结构，都离不开笔画。只有学会每一个笔画，才能掌握正确的书写方法。其次，只有了解汉字的笔画才能确定每个汉字基本的组成部分和偏旁部首，同时也有助于掌握笔画的变体。另外，无论查字典还是用电脑，往往也需要知道一个汉字有多少笔画以及它的起笔和收笔。

3. 笔画的类别

我们可以根据汉字中使用的单一笔画的区别来对笔画进行分类。汉字大约包括 30 多种不同的笔画。每种类型内部还有细微的差异。总的来说，汉字笔画可以分为两类：基本笔画和复合笔画。

（1）基本笔画

笔画的方向始终没有变化的称为基本笔画。比如，竖（丨）是一个基本笔画，因为它是一条线向一个方向移动的。传统的汉字基本笔画有 8 种，即：点（丶）、横（一）、竖（丨）、撇（丿）、捺（乀）、提（㇀）、折（𠃍）、钩（亅）。1965 年 1

were gradually determined.

2. The function of strokes

Understanding the strokes and stroke patterns of Chinese characters is critical when learning Chinese characters and calligraphy. Firstly, learners must know each stroke before learning stroke orders and the structures of characters. This ensures that the writer follows the correct way to write characters. Secondly, understanding individual strokes of a character can also help identify fundamental components and the radical of each character, as well as mastering variations of each stroke. In addition, the knowledge of strokes can help define beginning and ending strokes of a character and count the number of strokes within a character. This becomes necessary when using a dictionary or in computing.

3. Types of strokes

All single-stroke components that are used to write Chinese characters can be identified and classified based on their differences. There are around over thirty different types of strokes recognized in character writing, and each type of stroke has variations. In general, all strokes of Chinese characters can be classified into two categories: basic strokes and compound strokes.

(1) Basic strokes

A stroke whose direction remains the same is called a basic stroke. For example, vertical (丨) is classified as a basic stroke because it is a single stroke that forms one line moving in one direction. Traditionally, there

月 30 日中华人民共和国文化部和中国文字改革委员会发布的《印刷通用汉字字形表》和 1988 年 3 月国家语言文字工作委员会、中华人民共和国新闻出版署发布的《现代汉语通用字表》规定了 5 种基本笔画：横（一）、竖（丨）、撇（丿）、点（丶）、折（一），又称为"札字法"。

根据传统的分类，表 4-1 列出了 8 种基本笔画。这些基本笔画可以分为两组：单一型和附属型。单一型的基本笔画（如"横"和"点"）可以单独书写；而附属型的基本笔画（如"钩"）则不能单独出现，它必须跟至少一个笔画搭配组成一个结合型的笔画，因此这类基本笔画不是独立的笔画。

were eight basic strokes: dot (丶), horizontal (一), vertical (丨), left falling (丿), right falling (丶), raise (⼂), fold (一), and hook (丿). On January 30, 1965, the *General Chinese Character Form for Printing*, issued by the Ministry of Culture of the People's Republic of China and the Committee for Chinese Characters Reform, and *Table of Common Modern Chinese Characters* issued by the State Language Commission and China's National Press and Publication Administration in March 1988, stipulated five basic strokes: horizontal (一), vertical (丨), left falling (丿), dot (丶), and fold (一). This also became known as "Principles of Character *Zha* (札)".

Table 4-1 lists eight basic strokes based on traditional classification. These basic strokes can be divided into two stroke groups: simple and affiliated groups. Simple strokes (such as "horizontal" and "dot") can

表 4-1　汉字基本笔画
Table 4-1　Basic Strokes of Chinese Characters

基本笔画 Basic Stroke		名称 Name	例字 Sample Character
单一型 Simple Group	丶	点（diǎn）dot	六 广 义 头 家
	一	横（héng）horizontal	二 天 万 可 平
	丨	竖（shù）vertical	十 上 甲 中 出
	⼂	提（tí）raise	习 冲 冰 准 刁
	丶	捺（nà）right falling	八 大 人 夫 木
	丿	撇（piě）left falling	九 川 午 失 后
附属型 Affiliated Group	丿	钩（gōu）hook	了 小 衣 力 也
	一	折（zhé）fold	买 书 民 孔 室

（2）复合笔画

笔画方向发生变化的称为复合笔画。一个复合笔画由两个或两个以上的基本笔画组合而成，比如，"𠃌"（竖折折）是三个基本笔画的连续移动。表4-2列举了汉字的复合笔画。

be written alone. Affiliated strokes (such as "hook") never occur alone, but must be paired with at least one basic stroke to form an affiliated stroke. Thus, the affiliated stroke is not in itself an individual stroke.

(2) Compound strokes

A stroke whose direction changes is called a compound stroke. A compound stroke is produced when two or more basic strokes are combined. For example, "𠃌" is a sequence of three basic strokes written without lifting the writing instrument from the writing surface. Table 4-2 lists a selection of compound strokes of Chinese characters.

表4-2　汉字复合笔画
Table 4-2　Compound Strokes of Chinese Characters

序号 No.	复合笔画 Compound Stroke	名称 Name	例字 Sample Character
1	㇕	横折（héngzhé）	口 日 田 白 页
2	㇆	横折钩（héngzhégōu）	月 习 用 勺 为
3	㇊	横折提（héngzhétí）	计 说 话 语 谁
4	㇅	横折折（héngzhézhé）	凹
5	㇎	横折折折（héngzhézhézhé）	凸
6	㇡	横折折折钩（héngzhézhézhégōu）	乃 孕 仍 奶 扔
7	㇋	横折折撇（héngzhézhépiě）	建 及 吸 延 极
8	㇇	横钩（hénggōu）	买 写 卖 宝 家
9	㇇	横撇（héngpiě）	又 夕 径 双 受
10	㇌	横撇弯钩（héngpiěwāngōu）	队 邮 阳 阴 那
11	㇈	横折弯（héngzhéwān）	没 投 朵 役 躲
12	㇈	横折弯钩（héngzhéwāngōu）	九 几 亿 吃 艺

续表 Continued Table

序号 No.	复合笔画 Compound Stroke	名称 Name	例字 Sample Character
13	乙	横折斜钩（héngzhéxiégōu）	飞 气 风 汽 氧
14	㇃	卧钩（wògōu）	心 必 沁 志 怎
15	亅	竖钩（shùgōu）	争 事 求 水 到
16	㇙	竖提（shùtí）	以 比 切 良 民
17	㇄ ㇈	竖折（shùzhé）	山 区 世 牙 乐
18	㇅	竖折折（shùzhézhé）	专 鼎
19	㇉	竖折折钩（shùzhézhégōu）	亏 强 弓 与 马
20	㇋	竖弯（shùwān）	四 西 酒
21	㇄	竖弯钩（shùwāngōu）	儿 元 兄
22	㇗	竖折撇（shùzhépiě）	专 传 转
23	㇛	撇点（piědiǎn）	女 好 她
24	㇊	撇折（piězhé）	么 互 东
25	㇂	斜钩（xiégōu）	我 代 成
26	㇀	弯钩（wāngōu）	家 猫 狗

4.2 笔顺

大多数汉字有一个以上的笔画，有的汉字甚至超过25画。如果一个汉字有两个或两个以上的笔画，那么应该先写哪个笔画呢？笔画有没有书写的顺序呢？事实上，为了书写的自然和流畅，学习者必须按照笔画的顺序来书写，而笔画的顺序是有规律的。有些学习者往往忽视笔画的顺序，他们写汉字时好像是在

4.2 The Stroke Order

Most Chinese characters contain more than one stroke. Some Chinese characters even have over 25 strokes. If a Chinese character consists of two or more strokes, which stroke comes first? Is there a stroke order? As a matter of fact, in order to write naturally and fluently, learners must follow and write characters according to the stroke order rules, which is regular. Some learners often neglect the stroke order and seem to "draw" the character instead of "writing"

"画"字而不是在"写"字，结果，不仅容易丢掉汉字中的一些笔画，把汉字内部的结构打乱，而且字也写不好。可见，按照汉字的笔画顺序来书写是十分重要的。这样做不仅能帮助你记忆汉字，而且也能使你的字看起来更漂亮。

总的来说，学习者需要遵守 8 条有关笔顺的基本规则。

（1）先横后竖：当一个汉字又有横画又有竖画的时候，要先写横画或由横画组成的笔画，后写竖画或撇、捺。比如：十、干、下。

it. As a result, some strokes are missed, the structures of the Chinese characters are disordered, and the handwriting is generally poor. It can be seen that it is very important to follow the stroke order rules which can help memorize the characters and learn to write them beautifully.

In general, learners need to follow the eight basic rules of stroke order.

(1) Horizontal before vertical. When a Chinese character has both horizontal and vertical strokes, first write the "horizontal" stroke or the strokes consisting of horizontal strokes, then write the "vertical", "left falling", or "right falling" strokes, e.g., 十, 干 and 下.

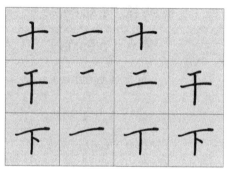

（2）先撇后捺：当撇和捺相交或相连时，先写撇，后写捺。比如：人、又、天。

(2) Left falling before right falling. When the "left falling" stroke and the "right falling" stroke cross or join each other, first write the "left falling" then the "right falling" stroke, e.g., 人, 又 and 天.

（3）先上后下：一般来说，先写上边的笔画，后写下边的笔画。比如：三、王、言。

(3) From top to bottom. Generally speaking, the upper stroke(s) should be written before lower stroke(s), e.g., 三, 王 and 言.

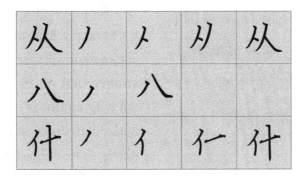

（4）先左后右：先写左边的笔画，后写右边的笔画。比如：从、八、什。

(4) From left to right. Write the stroke(s) on the left before the stroke(s) on the right, e.g., 从, 八 and 什.

（5）先外后内：当一个字上方有包围结构（包括左上方、右上方和左右上三方）时，先写外边的笔画，后写里边的笔画或被包围的笔画。比如：习、厌、同。

(5) From the outer to the inner. When a Chinese character has some strokes enclosed from the upper end (including upper left, upper right, and upper left to right), first write the enclosing strokes and then what is enclosed, e.g., 习, 厌 and 同.

但是，如果一个字下方有包围结构（包括左下方或左下右三方包围），则要先内后外。比如：送、凶、画。

However, if a character has some strokes enclosed from the lower end (including lower left or lower left to right), first write what is enclosed and then the enclosing strokes, e.g., 送, 凶 and 画.

（6）先进去，后关门：这是一个形象的说法。当一个字的四面都有包围笔画的时候，先写上方三面的包围笔画，再写被包围的笔画，最后写下面关门封口的横画，就像等人进去再关门一样。比如：因、目、回。

(6) Inside before closing the door. This is a figurative statement for the case when a character has some strokes completely enclosed on all four sides. Write the enclosing strokes first on the upper three sides, then what is enclosed, and finally the sealing horizontal stroke at the bottom. It is like the phrase "close the door after one has entered the room", e.g., 因, 目 and 回.

（7）先中间，后两边：当一个字的中间是以一竖画为中心，或者这个竖画与一横画相交时，先写中间，再写左右两边。比如：小、水、亚、木。

(7) The middle before two sides. When a vertical stroke of a character is in the middle, or when it crosses a horizontal stroke, it should be written first, e.g., 小, 水, 亚 and 木.

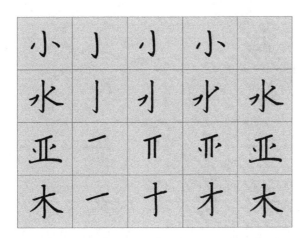

但是，如果中心的竖画和其他笔画相交，那么竖画则应后写。比如：中、丰、半。

However, when a middle vertical stroke crosses other strokes, it should be written last, e.g., 中, 丰 and 半.

（8）综合规则：上述7条规则都是最基本的，但不是绝对的，应该综合运用。比如：基本规则是先横后竖，但是如果竖出现在横的左边，则要先写竖，后写横，比如：上、仁。还有一种情况是，横画在中间或下边并且是主要笔画时，应该最后写，比如：子、女、且。

(8) The integrative rule. The seven rules above are the basic rules, but are by no means absolute. They should be applied in an integrative manner. For instance, the general rule is to write the horizontal stroke before the vertical stroke. But when the vertical stroke is on the left of the horizontal stroke, the vertical stroke precedes the horizontal stroke, e.g., 上 and 仁. Another case is when the horizontal stroke is in the middle, or at the bottom and takes prominent position, it should be written last, e.g., 子, 女 and 且.

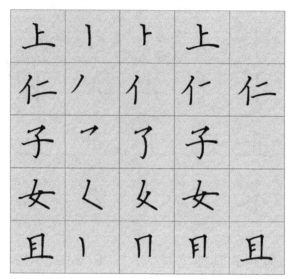

表4-3总结了上述8条规则：

Table 4-3 summarizes the above eight rules:

表4-3　汉字笔顺规则

Table 4-3　Stroke Order Rules of Chinese Characters

序号 No.	规则 Rule	例字 Sample Character	笔顺 Stroke Order
1	先横后竖 Horizontal before vertical	干	一 二 干
		丰	一 二 三 丰
2	先撇后捺 Left falling before right falling	人	丿 人
		大	一 ナ 大
3	先上后下 From top to bottom	三	一 二 三
		言	、 亠 言 言 言 言 言
4	先左后右 From left to right	从	丿 人 从 从
		明	丨 冂 日 日 日 明 明 明
5	先外后内 From the outer to the inner	同	丨 冂 冂 同 同 同
		问	、 丨 门 门 问 问
6	先进去，后关门 Inside before closing the door	田	丨 冂 日 田 田
		回	丨 冂 冂 冋 回 回

续表 Continued Table

序号 No.	规则 Rule	例字 Sample Character	笔顺 Stroke Order
7	先中间，后两边 The middle before two sides	小	亅 小 小
		水	亅 刂 水 水
8	综合规则 The integrative rule	上	丨 卜 上
		女	乚 夕 女

笔画的形成与笔顺的规则充分体现了汉字的线条艺术——自然流畅，平衡连贯，交错变化，浑然天成。每一个笔画都是造字的物质材料，通过它们之间的巧妙搭配，可以造出形态优美的汉字。每一个笔画也都倾注了造字者的想象力和抽象能力，以及他们对艺术的诠释、对客观世界的概括。汉字的一笔一画再现了自然之美，是形象艺术和抽象艺术的统一。

The formation of strokes and the rules of stroke order fully reflect the line art of Chinese characters—natural and smooth, balanced and coherent, interlaced and changed, and it is a natural unity. Each stroke is a material for creating characters, and through the ingenious combination between them, beautiful Chinese characters can be created. Each stroke is also poured into the imagination and abstraction of the creators, as well as their interpretation of art and a generalization of the objective world. Through one stroke, the beauty of nature is reproduced, which is the unity of graphic art and abstract art.

思考题 Questions

1. 传统上，数以万计的汉字是由几种基本笔画组成的？

2. 大多数汉字平均有多少笔画？

3. 为什么按照笔画的顺序书写汉字十分重要？

1. Traditionally, how many basic strokes that make up thousands of Chinese characters?

2. How many strokes on average do most Chinese characters contain?

3. Why is it important to follow the stroke order to write characters?

4. 当一个汉字又有横画又有竖画的时候，先写哪一笔？请举例说明。

5. 当一个汉字又有撇画又有捺画的时候，先写哪一笔？请举例说明。

6. 当一个汉字又有上边笔画又有下边笔画的时候，先写哪一笔？请举例说明。

7. 当一个汉字又有左边笔画又有右边笔画的时候，先写哪一笔？请举例说明。

8. 当一个汉字又有外边笔画又有里边笔画的时候，先写哪一笔？请举例说明。

9. 当一个汉字四边被围起来时，先写哪一笔？请举例说明。

10. 当一个汉字的中间以一个竖画为中心时，先写哪一笔？请举例说明。

11. 有关笔画顺序的基本规则是否在任何情况下都是固定不变的？

12. 汉字笔画与笔顺的规则是否体现了线条艺术？

4. Which stroke goes first if a character has both "horizontal" and "vertical" strokes? Please give examples.

5. Which stroke goes first if a character has both "left falling" and "right falling" strokes? Please give examples.

6. Which stroke goes first if a character has both "top" and "bottom" strokes? Please give examples.

7. Which stroke goes first if a character has both "left" and "right" strokes? Please give examples.

8. Which stroke goes first if a character has both "outer" and "inner" parts? Please give examples.

9. Which stroke goes first if a character is completely enclosed on all four sides? Please give examples.

10. Which stroke goes first if a character has a vertical stroke that is in the middle? Please give examples.

11. Are the rules of stroke order always fixed under any circumstances?

12. Do the strokes and rules of stroke order of Chinese characters reflect line art?

第五章　汉字的结构美
Chapter Five　The Structural Beauty of Chinese Characters

汉字是方块字，每个汉字的笔画和部首都需要均匀地分布在一个方块里，而如何分布则有一定的规律可循。汉字的结构一般可分为独体结构和合体结构，独体字数量较少，绝大部分是合体字。

5.1 独体字

这类汉字仅有一个独立的部件，即在形体上不能再分离出另一个表义或表音的字素。独体字尽管数量较少，但十分重要。大部分独体字不但使用频繁，而且也是合体字重要的构字部件。因此，我们不仅要会写会认这些常用的独体字，而且要反复练习，尽量把这些字写得端正漂亮。比如：

5.2 合体字

大多数汉字是由两个或两个以上的部件构成的，也就是至少包括两个表音

Chinese characters are known as square-shaped characters. The strokes and radicals of each character are placed proportionally within the square and the placement is governed by rules. The structures of Chinese characters can be roughly divided into single structure and compound structure. Single characters only consist of a small portion of the Chinese characters; the vast majority of the characters are compound characters.

5.1 Single Characters

This type of character only consists of one independent component that can not be divided into a morpheme meaningfully or phonetically. Despite the small number of single characters, they are important. Most of them are frequently used and also function as the components of compound characters. Therefore, we should not only be able to write and read these commonly used single characters, but also write these characters beautifully by practicing them repeatedly. Look at the examples on the left.

5.2 Compound Characters

Most Chinese characters are composed of two or more components, that is a character consists of at least two morphemes meaningfully or phonetically. Due to its structure, such a Chinese character is called a

或表义的字素。这样的汉字从结构上可称为合体字。合体字中以左右结构和上下结构为主。

在所有的汉字中，左右结构的汉字最多，上下结构的汉字次之。这两种结构的汉字大约占汉字总数的85%。因此，如果能掌握这两种汉字结构的书写方法，就等于掌握了大多数汉字的书写方法。

（1）左右结构

左右结构的汉字包括左边和右边两个组字的部件。根据左边部件和右边部件的相对大小，这种结构的汉字又可以分为三个小类：

I. 左小右大

compound character. The majority of compound characters are left-right or top-bottom structures.

Of all the characters, those with left-right structures are more numerous than those with top-bottom structures. Characters of these two structures approximately account for 85% of all Chinese characters. Therefore, if you have gained mastery over the writing methods of these two main structures, you will gain mastery over the writing methods of most Chinese characters.

(1) Left-right structure

Chinese characters of this structure consist of a left part and a right part. On the basis of the relative size of the left and right parts, it can be subdivided into three sub-structures:

I. A smaller left part plus a larger right part

II. 左右两部分基本一样大

II. Two parts of roughly equal size

III. 左大右小

III. A larger left part plus a smaller right part

（2）上下结构

基于同样的原因，上下结构的汉字也有三个小类：

I. 上小下大

(2) Top-bottom structure

As in the left-right structure, three sub-structures can be found in the top-bottom structure:

I. A shorter top part plus a longer bottom part

II. 上下两部分基本一样大

II. Two parts of roughly equal length

III. 上大下小

III. A longer top part plus a shorter bottom part

（3）包围结构

除了左右结构和上下结构之外，汉字还有另外一种结构——包围结构。这种结构也可分为三个小类：

I. 两边包围结构

① 从左边和上边包围

② 从上边和右边包围

③ 从左边和下边包围

II. 三边包围结构

① 从左、上、右三边包围

(3) Enclosed structure

In addition to the left-right and top-bottom structures, Chinese characters have another structure: enclosed structure. It can also be subdivided into three sub-structures:

I. Enclosed on two sides

① Enclosed from the upper left

② Enclosed from the upper right

③ Enclosed from the lower left

II. Enclosed from three sides

① Enclosed from left, top and right

② 从上、左、下三边包围

② Enclosed from top, left and bottom

③ 从左、下、右三边包围

③ Enclosed from left, bottom and right

III. 四面全包围结构

III. Enclosed from all four sides

一个汉字就像是一座建筑，既要美观又要匀称。因此，如果要把汉字写漂亮，就必须注意到每一个汉字的内部结构。构字部件之间要保持平衡，即笔画多的部件一般要比笔画少的占用更大的空间。我们可以根据构字部件的情况，把一个汉字所占据的空间分成几份。比如，一个左右结构的汉字，如果它右边的部件大，左边的部件小，那么就可给大部件三分之二的空间，而小部件只需要三分之一的空间。如果两个部件大小

A Chinese character is just like a building with an aim of beauty and symmetry. Therefore, if you want to write them beautifully, you must pay attention to its structure of each character. The components should be well-balanced, that is, the component with more strokes should take up a larger space than the one with fewer strokes. The space taken up by a character can be divided into several parts according to its components. For instance, if a left-right structured character has a larger right part, then the right part should take up two-thirds of the space, the left part should take one-third. If both parts are of similar size, roughly

相似，那么每个部件所占的空间就基本相等。这就是为什么练习书法时初学者往往要使用米字格或九宫格的原因。

5.3 偏旁与部首

大部分汉字都是由几个部件组成的，而其中绝大多数汉字是形声字。形声字包括两个部件或偏旁：表示意义的偏旁（义符）和表示读音的偏旁（声符）。由于义符和声符结合起来能表示一个汉字的意义和读音，所以掌握它们十分重要。在学习汉字的过程中，学习者会逐步意识到这些偏旁的重要性，并初步了解偏旁与汉字之间的关系。需要注意的是，由于语言的变化等各种原因，并不是所有的义符都跟由它所组成的汉字的意思有关，并非所有的声符都跟带有它的汉字的读音有关，我们不能把这些符号的作用绝对化、静止化。汉语有几千年的历史，汉字自然也不可避免地发生了不少变化。

所以，如果某一个偏旁在表义或表音方面作用明显，与所构成的汉字的字义或字音联系紧密，那么就尽量利用这个偏旁来学习汉字；相反，如果一个偏旁与含有这个偏旁的汉字之间找不到直

equal space should be allocated. This is why when practicing calligraphy beginners often use workbooks with guidelines of 米 or nine square grid.

5.3 The Components and Radicals

The majority of Chinese characters consist of several components and most of them are pictophonetic characters. They have two components or radicals: the meaning component (or "meaning radical") and the phonetic component (or "phonetic radical"). Since the two components of a character explain both meaning and sound, it is important to master them. During the course of learning Chinese characters, learners will gradually realize the importance of these components and have a preliminary understanding of the relationship between character and its components. Take note that, due to the evolution of the language, not all Chinese characters are related to their meaning components, nor are they necessarily related to their phonetic components in sound. Make sure to avoid taking the role of these components as absolute and static. Chinese language has a history of thousands of years and the characters have inevitably changed over time.

Therefore, if a radical plays an obvious role in expressing meaning or pronunciation and is closely related to the meaning or pronunciation of the Chinese character, make full use of this radical to learn the characters. On the contrary, when it is not, do not go to

接联系，那就不要去钻牛角尖，硬性地把偏旁和汉字的字音、字义联系起来。总之，最终的目的是会认、会写这个汉字，而且能写得美观。

表 5-1 中是 50 个独体字。它们也是组字部件，在字典中被称为"部首"。可以说，每个部首最初都是独体字。随着汉字字形的变化，有些部首不能单独作为独体字使用了；有些独体字还能作为部首使用，但随着汉字的简化，形体上发生了变化。

the extreme and rigidly connect the radical with the sound and meaning of the Chinese character. In short, the final aim is to be able to remember the character, read it, and write it beautifully.

Table 5-1 lists 50 single characters that are also components of characters. They are designated "radicals" in the dictionary. It could be said that each radical was originally a single character. With the evolution of Chinese character pattern, some radicals are no longer used as single characters. Others are still used as radicals, but they have changed their forms with the simplification of Chinese characters.

表 5-1　汉字常用部首 50 个
Table 5-1　50 Commonly Used Radicals in Chinese Characters

序号 No.	现代字形 Modern Character Form	图示 Drawing	古代字形 Ancient Character Form	字义 Meaning	发音 Pronunciation
1	人			person	rén
2	刀			knife	dāo
3	力			power/strength	lì
4	又			right hand/again	yòu
5	大			big	dà

续表 Continued Table

序号 No.	现代字形 Modern Character Form	图示 Drawing	古代字形 Ancient Character Form	字义 Meaning	发音 Pronunciation
6	女	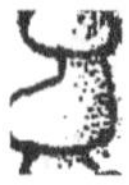	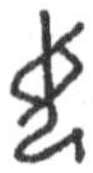	female	nǚ
7	子	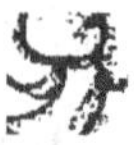	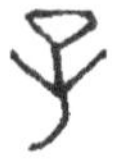	son/child	zǐ
8	寸	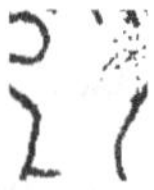	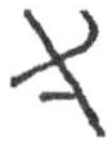	*a unit for measuring length*	cùn
9	口	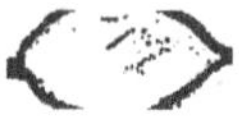	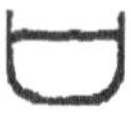	mouth	kǒu
10	囗	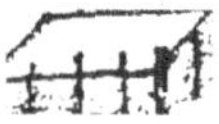		to enclose	wéi
11	土		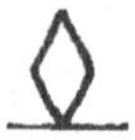	soil/earth	tǔ
12	小	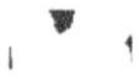	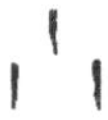	small	xiǎo
13	干	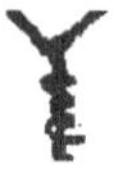	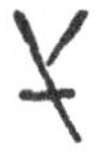	trunk/dry	gàn/gān
14	工	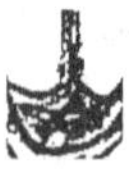	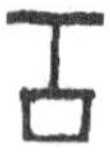	tool/work	gōng
15	山	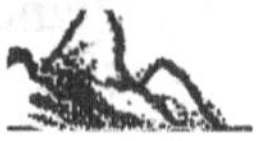	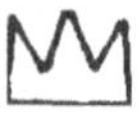	mountain	shān
16	巾	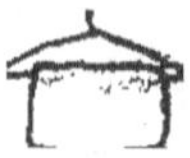	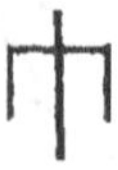	a piece of cloth	jīn

续表 Continued Table

序号 No.	现代字形 Modern Character Form	图示 Drawing	古代字形 Ancient Character Form	字义 Meaning	发音 Pronunciation
17	门			door	mén
18	马			horse	mǎ
19	弓			bow	gōng
20	幺			tiny	yāo
21	广			wide	guǎng
22	手			hand	shǒu
23	木			wood/tree	mù
24	火			fire	huǒ
25	水			water	shuǐ
26	心			heart	xīn
27	日		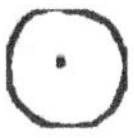	sun	rì

续表 Continued Table

序号 No.	现代字形 Modern Character Form	图示 Drawing	古代字形 Ancient Character Form	字义 Meaning	发音 Pronunciation
28	月			moon	yuè
29	贝			shell	bèi
30	车			cart/vehicle	chē
31	文			script	wén
32	王			king	wáng
33	长			long/old	cháng/zhǎng
34	目			eye	mù
35	田			field	tián
36	石			rock	shí
37	立			to stand	lì
38	鸟			bird	niǎo

续表　Continued Table

序号 No.	现代字形 Modern Character Form	图示 Drawing	古代字形 Ancient Character Form	字义 Meaning	发音 Pronunciation
39	穴			cave	xué
40	示			to show	shì
41	虫			worm/insect	chóng
42	肉			meat/flesh	ròu
43	竹			bamboo	zhú
44	衣			clothing	yī
45	米			rice	mǐ
46	言			speech	yán
47	糸			fine silk	mì
48	走			to run	zǒu
49	金			gold/metal	jīn

续表 Continued Table

序号 No.	现代字形 Modern Character Form	图示 Drawing	古代字形 Ancient Character Form	字义 Meaning	发音 Pronunciation
50	雨			rain	yǔ

汉字的结构，无论是上下结构，还是左右结构或包围结构，都端正大方，搭配匀称，疏密得当，充满立体感——以静示动，寓静于动，以搭配示平衡，以组合示统一，在固定的结构中展现了朴素的审美意识，再现了空间艺术和视觉艺术。每种结构都取于自然，还于自然，带有大自然的神韵。

The structures of Chinese characters, whether it is the top-bottom structure, the left-right structure or the enclosed structure, are all upright, generous, well-proportioned, well-spaced, and full of three-dimensionality—showing motion by static state and moving by static state, showing balance by stroke matching, showing unity by stroke combination. The simple aesthetic consciousness is displayed in the fixed structure, and the space art and visual art are reproduced. Each structure is taken from nature and returns to nature with the charm of nature.

思考题 Questions

1. 一个汉字的笔画和部首应该怎样分布？

2. 汉字的结构有几种？请举例说明。

3. 合体字有几种主要结构？

4. 85% 的汉字属于哪些结构？

5. 左右结构的汉字可以分为几个小类？

1. How should the stroke(s) and component of a Chinese character be placed?

2. How are Chinese characters divided based on their structures? Please give examples.

3. How many major structures are there in compound characters?

4. What are the structures that 85% of all Chinese characters belong to?

6. 上下结构的汉字可以分为几个小类？

7. 包围结构的汉字可以分为几个小类？

8. "女"是一个独体字，但是在合体字中也可以是一个组字部件。请用"女"做部首组成两个合体字。

9. "问"是一个合体字，请把它分成两个独体字。

10. 你认为汉字的结构美不美？为什么？请举例说明。

5. What are the sub-categories under the left-right structure?

6. What are the sub-categories under the top-bottom structure?

7. What are the sub-categories under the enclosed structure?

8. "女" is a single character, but it can also be a component in a compound character. Please use "女" as a component/radical to form two compound characters.

9. "问" is a compound character. Please divide it into two single characters.

10. Do you think the structure of Chinese characters is beautiful? Why? Please give examples.

第六章　汉字的艺术价值
Chapter Six　The Artistic Value of Chinese Characters

汉字作为一种语言文字，记录下了丰富多彩的历史进程和社会变迁。在五千年的中华文明中，汉字随着历史文明一起发展，经历了多次演变和进化，逐渐成熟，日臻完善。可以说，汉字的历史和中国的历史相互关联、相互依存。汉字的造字法包括了象形、指事、会意、形声、假借、转注等"六书"，具有鲜明的形象色彩。汉字的造型不仅展现了中华民族的创造力量，而且升华为一种卓越的视觉造型艺术。

6.1 汉字的造型艺术

汉字是视觉艺术与民族文化的结合，凝聚着中华民族的想象力与艺术创造力。在当今全球化和信息化的背景下，汉字依然展示着中国人的审美观、价值观、联想力和创造力，彰显着中华文化的特质，并为多元性的世界文化贡献了中国人的智慧和理念。汉字的造型艺术可以从下面三个方面来分析。

1. 汉字结构的唯美性

汉字是由点、线等笔画构成的，本

As a written language, Chinese characters have recorded a colorful history and changing society. During the 5,000 years of Chinese civilization, Chinese characters developed along with Chinese civilization and underwent many evolutions, gradually being mature and perfect. It could be said that the history of Chinese characters and Chinese history are intertwined and interdependent. Chinese characters are classified within the "six categories", including pictographic, indicative, suggestive, pictophonetic, borrowed and etymological characters. The bright and distinctive graphic design of Chinese characters can not only show the creative power of the Chinese nation, but also sublimate the structure of Chinese characters into an outstanding visual example of artistry.

6.1 The Artistic Structure of Characters

Chinese characters, as a combination of a visual art and national culture, embody the imagination and artistic creativity of the Chinese nation. In the context of globalization and informationization, Chinese characters still demonstrate the Chinese people's aesthetics, ideology, imagination, creative power and the special nature of Chinese culture, contributing Chinese people's wisdom and ideas to the diversification of world culture. The artistic structure of characters can

身就具有美学的因素。点和线组成文字，如同用建筑材料盖房子，形成了复杂的二维图画式结构，它不仅能传达信息，也能展现美感。汉字符号能使人们在识别字义的同时获得美的感受。汉字之美表现在笔形字形、间架结构上，是汉字局部、汉字个体与汉字之间的和谐统一。汉字书写必须体现汉字所具有的节奏感和韵律感，强调笔画的组合与搭配，以及部首与部首、汉字与汉字之间的对比与统一。汉字的造型源于自然，也自然地展示出了美学表现力。（图 6-1）

图 6-1 清代康熙皇帝题写的"福"字
Figure 6-1 Character "*Fu* (blessing)" written by Emperor Kangxi of the Qing Dynasty

2. 汉字结构的独特性

汉字来源于象形文字，并始终保留

be viewed from the following three aspects.

1. The Aesthetic Structure of Characters

Chinese characters are composed of strokes, including dots and lines, which are aesthetic elements by themselves—like building a house with building materials. Strokes can create complex two-dimensional pictorial structures that convey both information and beauty. The design of Chinese characters can not only provide readers with the meaning of the character, but also gives them aesthetic recognition. The beauty of Chinese characters is found in both the structure of strokes and the unity of characters. Writing characters must reflect their sense of rhythm, emphasizing the combination and collocation of strokes, as well as the contrast and unity of radicals and individual characters. The structure of characters is originally based on nature, and it naturally shows a aesthetic expression. (Figure 6-1)

2. The Distinguishing Structure of Characters

Chinese characters are based on and still possess some of the features of pictographic characters that are very different from the written forms of other languages. Chinese characters maintain a sense of continuity while giving each character its own unique identity. Each character in graphic design also has a unique visual representation with a unique personality, power, and history that creates a personalized visual appeal.

3. The Creative Structure of Characters

Chinese characters themselves are a dual carrier of language and art. They

着象形文字的一些特点，因而与其他文字的字体特征有着明显的区别。汉字在整体上有其共性，同时，每个汉字也各自具有独特的字体结构和特征，具有自身的个性、力量和历史，富有个性化的视觉感染力。

3. 汉字结构的创造性

汉字本身是语言和艺术的双重载体。记录和传递信息是汉字生命的本源，而字形的结构艺术则更体现了汉字的魅力。每个汉字都是艺术性的创造。汉字本身奇妙的结构、丰富的内涵、对文化和历史的传承，都使汉字成为进行艺术创作的理想素材。汉字字义、字形和字音的结合能产生强烈的感染力和冲击力，而形体美、韵律美、意境美也使得汉字在现代设计中得到了更广泛的应用。

6.2 汉字的形、音、义

1. 形美如画

汉字不仅具有造型美，而且通过造型反映出了中国古人朴素的审美意识。

首先，汉字的结构强调和谐对称。很多汉字都是由对称的结构组成的。比如，双"木"组成"林"字，左右对称；三个"木"组成"森"字，也是匀称的。

originated merely as a means of recording and communicating information. However, the structural artistry reflects the charm of characters. Each character is an artistic creation. The marvelous structure of Chinese characters, their complicated connotations, and the inheritance of history and culture all make them the ideal writing materials for artistic creation. The combination of a Chinese character's meaning, shape, and sound can produce strong appeal and impact. This combination of beauty of shape, rhythm, and artistic conception has gone on to be widely used in contemporary designs.

6.2 The "Shape, Sound and Meaning" of Chinese Characters

1. The Shape of a Chinese Character is as Beautiful as a Picture

Chinese characters not only have a beautiful shape, they also reflect the simple aesthetic consciousness of ancient Chinese people.

Firstly, the structure of Chinese characters places special importance on harmony and symmetry. Many Chinese characters are formed on symmetrical structures. For example, combining two of the character "木 (*Mu*, wood/tree)" creates the character "林 (*Lin*, woods)", which is symmetrical; combining three "木" creates "森 (*Sen*, forest)", which is also symmetrical. The character "朋 (*Peng*, friend)" consists of two "月 (*Yue*, moon)", which structurally represents the harmony between two friends.

"朋"字则由两个"月"组成，从结构上表现了友人之间的和谐关系。这种由两个或三个相同字符组成的会意字，不仅表示了新的意思，而且给人带来匀称和谐的审美感受。

其次，汉字造型具有形象性。比如，"雨"字让人仿佛看到雨水从天而降，"水"字使人感受到水的流动，"羊"字勾画出羊的头部轮廓，"牢"字令人联想到牛关在窄小的屋檐下。

最后，汉字造型端庄大气，具有形体美。汉字虽然分为上下结构、左右结构和包围结构等多种结构，但是都具有搭配变化的美感。汉字从形体上看都是"方块字"，方方正正，端正大气，如同人虽有胖瘦高矮之分，但是人体各部分都搭配得当，浑然一体。以"思""休""国"等字为例，"思"为上下结构，心的田野，用来表示人的思考之深或思念之情；"休"为左右结构，人依木而息，有停靠、休息之义；"国"为包围结构，国界之内蕴藏美玉宝藏，象征疆土完整，资源丰富，为立国之要素。虽然每个字造型各异，但都显得稳重端庄，各个造字部件合理搭配，完美结合，既巧妙地表现了字义，又匀称地展现了

These suggestive characters that consist of two or three identical parts not only represent a new meaning, but also bring a sense of harmony and aesthetic balance.

Secondly, the structure of Chinese characters is visual, such as the character "雨 (*Yu*, rain)" which conjures up the image of rain falling from the sky; the character "水 (*Shui*, water)" elicits the feeling of the flow of water; the character "羊 (*Yang*, sheep)" outlines the head of the sheep; the character "牢 (*Lao*, prison)" is reminiscent of a cow immobilized under a narrow eave.

Finally, Chinese characters are modeled with a dignified atmosphere and the beauty of shape. Although Chinese characters have top-bottom structure, left-right structure, enclosed structure and so on, they have the beauty of arrangement and change. The shapes of Chinese characters are all so-called "square characters". Like the human body, though there are fat, thin, high, and low people, all parts of the human body are properly matched and integrated seamlessly. For example, "思 (*Si*, to think)", "休 (*Xiu*, to rest)", and "国 (*Guo*, country/kingdom)". "思" has an upper structure (meaning "field") and a lower structure (meaning "heart"), together, the field of the heart, representing the depth of thinking and missing of people. "休" has a left structure (meaning "person") and a right structure (meaning "wood/tree"), together, a person leaning on a tree, meaning to stop and rest. "国" has an enclosed structure, the inside meaning the treasures of jade and the

形体，使字义有呼之欲出的感觉。

2. 音美如歌

汉字的构造精巧神奇，读音也同样美得令人陶醉。那些独立的音节如同乐曲的音符，形成美的节奏，回荡着美的旋律。它们或高或低，或长或短，错落有致，抑扬顿挫。细细品味，让人有一种身临其境的感觉，仿佛流水从身边流过，耳边回荡着哗哗的响声；似乎在群山之间，眼前出现了一幅美丽的景色，顿时令人心旷神怡。每一个汉字就如同一件精美的艺术品，风姿独秀，让人沉醉其间。

𰻞（音"biáng"，用于"biángbiáng面"）是一个合字，笔画繁多，难以用电脑输入。"biángbiáng面"是陕西传统风味面食，又名裤带面，特指用关中麦子磨成的面粉制作、手工拉成的又长又宽又厚的面条。这么复杂的汉字，为什么要念作 biáng 呢？有的人认为，biáng 的发音源于妇女洗衣服时用棒槌捶打湿衣服发出的声音；有的人认为，这是模仿面条制作过程中在案板上发出的 biángbiáng 的声音；还有人认为，调拌面条和面条入口后发出的声音听起来像 biángbiáng。这种响亮而浑厚的

outside meaning the national boundaries that protect it, symbolizing the integrity of the territory and the rich resources. Although each character has a different shape, they are all stable and dignified. The components of each character are matched with each other and perfectly combined to not only subtly express the meaning of the character, but also to show the shape and balance to create a vivid portrayal.

2. The Sound of a Chinese Character is as Melodious as a Song

The construction of Chinese characters is exquisite and magical, and the pronunciation is equally beautiful. Each independent syllable, like unique musical notes, emits a beautiful rhythm and echoes the beautiful melody. The tone of each syllable is either high or low, long or short, arranged irregularly or with swaying cadence. When you relish the sound, there is an immersive feeling—the sound of flowing water echoes in your ear. There is a refreshing, beautiful scene laid out in front of you as if you are in the mountains. Each character is like a beautiful piece of artwork, graceful and intoxicating.

𰻞 (*Biang*, as in *Biangbiangmian*) is a compound character with many strokes, which is difficult to be typed on a standard computer. *Biangbiangmian* refers to a kind of traditional noodles in Shaanxi Province, also known as "belt noodles". Usually, they are long, wide, and thick noodles handmade from wheat. Why is this complicated character pronounced as *biáng*? Some scholars believe that the biángbiáng 声也就成了"biángbiáng 面"名称的由来。总之，从中可以看到汉字的发音来自生活，带有自然的朴素的美。

3. 意美如诗

汉字不仅造型美、声音美，而且寓意美，蕴含了中国深邃的哲学思想。比如"仙"字，由"人"和"山"构成。为什么人在山中就是仙？因为人要是能摆脱市井尘世的困扰，便能无忧无虑了。其中暗含的意思是，仙其实也是人，不过是一些内在修为高、超凡脱俗的人。又如"看"字，上面是个"手"字，下面是个"目"字，意思是手放在眼睛上，搭成"凉棚"，为的是看得远、看得清。这也暗示着无论做人还是做事，都要眼光长远，不要鼠目寸光。再如，为什么"易"字表示变化呢？"易"上面是个"日"字，下面其实是个"月"字，日月交替，白天和夜晚循环往复，所以"易"其实是指日月的变化，也可以表示世界每天都处在变化之中。

中国汉字讲究以字传神。虽然世界上的万事万物纷繁复杂，千变万化，但是中国哲学强调化繁为简，一以贯之，用最简明、最直观的原始材料来表达最基本的规律和道理。汉字完美地体现了这种朴素的哲学观念。比如"仁"字，

pronunciation of *biáng* may come from the sound of women washing clothes with a wooden stick; some of them think that the process of making noodles on the board would produce a *biángbiáng* sound; and others believe that the character's pronunciation comes from the *biángbiáng* sounds while mixing and eating the noodles. The name of *Biangbiang* noodles is derived from this loud and vigorous *biángbiáng* sound. In short, it can be seen that the pronunciation of Chinese characters comes from life, with the simplicity of natural beauty.

3. The Meaning of a Chinese Character is as Poetic as a Poem

Chinese characters not only have a beautiful shape and sound but also contain the beauty of implied meaning and deep philosophical thoughts of Chinese culture. For instance, the Chinese character "仙 (*Xian*)" means "immortal", with the left part representing a person, and the right part representing a mountain. Why is a person in the mountain considered an immortal? Because the person is out of the chaotic street life and allowed to be carefree. It implies that an immortal is also a person, but he or she can initiate otherworldly personal growth. For instance, the character "看 (*Kan*, to look)" is comprised of a "hand" and an "eye"—put a hand over the eyes to cover the light, so that you can see things far away from you. This mirrors life's philosophy—a productive life requires foresight, don't let a leaf block your vision. Why does the character "易

用"人"和"二"两个部分表现了这个
重要的观念。《说文解字》解释："仁者，
亲也。从人二。"《中庸》解释："仁者，
人也。"简单地说，"仁"字象征的就是为
人之道，即做人要有爱心，与他人保持
平等，和谐相处。"二"这个抽象的符号
把这个道理表现得深入浅出，淋漓尽致。

6.3 汉字体现的"真、善、美"

中国道家创始人老子说："人法地，
地法天，天法道，道法自然。"这段话生
动地阐明了人类想象力、创造力的来源，
也成为人们审美观和艺术创作的依据。
中国汉字正是通过字形、字义和字音来
表现人们对自然的了解与认识，表现自
然之美的。自然之美可以概括为"真、
善、美"，无论是我们的生活，还是我们
的道德和精神，都可以用"真、善、美"
来衡量。具有"真"和"善"，才会产生
"美"。汉字作为记录汉语的工具，在形
式和内涵上都体现了"真、善、美"的
艺术价值。汉字艺术的"真"体现在人
们对自然万事万物的真切观察上，并用
汉字将其真实而抽象地呈现出来，既具
体又凝练，既形象又立体，静态和动感
相统一，把自然的真实升华为艺术的真

(*Yi*)" mean "to change"? The top part of the character "易" is "sun" and the bottom part means "moon". Because the sun and the moon alternate, day and night cycle, "易" refers to the change of the sun and the moon, and indicates that the world is changing every day.

Chinese characters are designed to use shape to show the literal and semantic meanings behind the characters. Although everything in the world is complicated and constantly changing, Chinese philosophical thought emphasizes simplicity. It uses the most concise and intuitive raw materials to express the most basic laws and principles. Chinese characters perfectly embody this simple philosophical concept. For example, "仁 (*Ren*, humanity/benevolence)" uses two parts, "亻" and "二" to express this important concept. *Shuowen Jiezi* explains: "Humanity means love and benevolence". *The Doctrine of the Mean* also explains: "The benevolent ones show humanity." Simply put, the character "仁" symbolizes the quality of humanity. A person must have love, maintain equality with others, and live in harmony. The abstract symbol "二" expresses this truth vividly.

6.3 "Truth, Kindness and Beauty" Reflected in Chinese Characters

Laozi, the ancestor of the Chinese Taoism, said, "Man follows the earth, the earth follows the heaven, the heaven follows the Tao (the Way), and the Tao (the Way) follows the nature." This passage vividly clarifies the source of human's imagination and creativity, and points out that people's aesthetic and

实，把"真"化为"美"。汉字艺术的"善"体现在人们对自然和人性的认知和理解上，通过笔画和部首的组合，人们把对道德的评判渗透到汉字中，诠释质朴的愿望和追求，展示美好的立意和心灵，化"善"为"美"。比如，什么是"好"？汉字用"女"和"子"的完美组合表示家庭和睦，琴瑟相合。再如，怎么表示"和谐"之"和"？汉字把"禾"与"口"组合起来，寓意谷物丰登，丰衣足食，国泰民安。汉字艺术的"美"在于它再现了大自然左右平衡、高低交替、阴阳融合、方正饱满、大气祥和的神韵。"真、善、美"相互交融，真即善，善即美，美即真。汉字艺术不仅反映了造字者的审美水准，而且也符合并满足了汉字使用者的审美需求，为大众展示了一件件精致的艺术品。（图6-2）

图6-2　很多书法家喜欢用"真善美"
三字来进行创作
Figure 6-2　Many calligraphers like to use three characters "truth, kindness and beauty" to create.

artistic creation are in accordance with the nature. Chinese characters have demonstrated Chinese people's knowledge and understanding of nature through the shape, meaning and sound, and presented the beauty of nature. The beauty of nature can be summarized as "truth, kindness, and beauty". No matter our daily life, or our morality and spirit, it can be measured by "truth, kindness, and beauty". Only with "truth" and "kindness" can "beauty" be produced. As a tool to record Chinese language, Chinese characters embody the artistic value of "truth, kindness and beauty" in their forms and connotations. The "truth" of Chinese characters is embodied in people's observation of nature, and it is presented in a true and abstract manner. Chinese characters are both concrete and concise, vivid and three-dimensional, static and dynamic, sublimating the truth of nature into the truth of art and turning "truth" into "beauty". The "kindness" of Chinese characters is reflected in people's cognition and understanding of nature and humanity. Through the combination of strokes and radicals, people's moral judgment is reflected by Chinese characters, interpreting people's simple wishes and pursuit, showing their beautiful conception and soul, and turning "kindness" into "beauty". For example, what is "好 (Hao, good)"? The Chinese character has the perfect combination of "女 (Nu, female)" and "子 (Zi, son/child)" to express harmony and balance in family and society. How to express "和 (He, harmony)"? The

2014 年 4 月 29 日，时任中国驻美大使崔天凯在出席美国威尔逊中心基辛格美中关系研究所新标志启用仪式后，决定送给基辛格博士一份特殊的礼物，以感谢他为中美关系发展做出的贡献。经过认真考虑，崔大使手写了一个汉字"基"，亲手送给基辛格博士（图 6-3）。崔天凯说："汉字'基'不仅是基辛格博士中文名字的第一个字，在中文中还有'基础''基本''重要'等很多含义。我认为这些含义用在基辛格博士身上非常合适。"我们从中可以看到，一个汉字可以蕴含很多美好的意义。

图 6-3　崔天凯大使为基辛格题写汉字"基"
Figure 6-3　Ambassador Cui Tiankai inscribed the Chinese character *Ji* for Dr. Kissinger.

Chinese character has the combination of "禾 (*He*, grain/crop)" and "口 (*Kou*, mouth)" to indicate that foods are abundant and harmony is achieved. The "beauty" of Chinese characters is presented by the balance of left and right or top and bottom, fusion of *Yin* and *Yang*, square corners and fullness with the natural rhyme. "Truth, kindness, and beauty" blend together; "truth" is "kindness", "kindness" is "beauty", and "beauty" is "truth". The art of Chinese characters not only reflects the aesthetic standards of the creators, but also meets and satisfies the aesthetic needs of users of Chinese characters, displaying pieces of precious artworks to the public. (Figure 6-2)

When Mr. Cui Tiankai, Chinese ambassador to the United States, attended the New Logo Opening Ceremony for Kissinger US-China Relations Institute of Wilson Center of USA on April 29, 2014, he decided to present Dr. Kissinger a special gift to thank him for his contribution to Sino-US relations. After careful consideration, Mr. Cui Tiankai wrote only one Chinese character "基 (*Ji*, base)" and presented it personally to Dr. Kissinger (Figure 6-3). Mr. Cui said that the Chinese character "基" not only was the first character in Dr. Kissinger's Chinese name, but also had other implications in Chinese language, including "foundation", "basic", and "important". All of these meanings, Mr. Cui believed, were suitable for Dr. Kissinger. We can also see from this example that a Chinese character can contain many beautiful conceptions.

思考题 Questions

1. 汉字是由笔画构成的，它本身具有美学的因素吗？为什么？

2. 为什么说汉字跟其他文字的字体具有明显的区别？

3. 为什么汉字能成为理想的进行艺术创作的素材？

4. 为什么说汉字"形美如画"？

5. 为什么说汉字"音美如歌"？

6. 为什么说汉字"意美如诗"？

7. 什么是"真、善、美"？

8. 你觉得汉字体现了"真、善、美"吗？

9. 你觉得汉字是怎样表现"美"的？

10. 你最喜欢哪一个汉字？为什么？

1. Chinese characters are composed of strokes. Do they have aesthetic factors themselves? Why?

2. Why is the font of Chinese characters different from other writing systems?

3. Why are Chinese characters ideal materials for artistic creation?

4. Why do we say "the shape of a Chinese character is as beautiful as a picture"?

5. Why do we say "the sound of a Chinese character is as melodious as a song"?

6. Why do we say "the meaning of a Chinese character is as poetic as a poem"?

7. What is "truth, kindness and beauty"?

8. Do you think "truth, kindness and beauty" appear in Chinese characters?

9. How do you think Chinese characters express "beauty"?

10. Which Chinese character do you like most? Why?

UNIT TWO 第二单元 2

The Art of Character Writing 书写艺术

第七章　中国书法及其历史源流
Chapter Seven　Chinese Calligraphy and Its History

7.1 什么是中国书法

书法就是书写的艺术。英文中"calligraphy"（书法）一词起源于希腊语，表示"好的"或"美丽的"书写。"好的"书写至少包含两个方面的意思：首先是书写的形式要正确，是约定俗成的语言符号，得到使用同一种语言的大众的认可；其次是要把各种符号协调地组合到一起，通过自然和谐的书写形式，使人们得到视觉上和精神上的享受。书法所表现出来的艺术魅力是无穷的。

据统计，世界上至少有 1000 种以上的书写系统或书面语。在起始阶段，书面语的作用是记下某个事件或当时当地人们的言行。人们书写的时候会尽量用不同的方式把书写的符号和语义、语音联系起来，由此创造出的书写系统也各不相同。有些语言的书面语注重拼写和读音的联系，而有些则把书写符号和意思紧密联系起来。总的来说，世界上有三种书写系统：（1）表音系统，如英文的字母；（2）音节系统，如日文的音节符号——假名；（3）表意系统，如中文的

7.1 What Is Chinese Calligraphy

Calligraphy is writing as an art. The term "calligraphy" in English derives from the Greek language, indicating "good" or "beautiful" writing. "Good" writing contains at least two aspects: (1) a sure knowledge of the correct form of writing, i.e., the conventional sign that is recognized by people who use the same language; and (2) the skill to inscribe them with a harmonious ordering of various parts, so that people will have visual and spiritual enjoyment. The artistic charm that calligraphy demonstrates is boundless.

According to the statistics, there are at least more than 1,000 kinds of writing systems or written languages in the world. At the beginning, the function of written language was to record events and what people did and said then and there. In writing, people strived in different ways to connect the writing symbols with meanings and sounds; therefore, the creation of written systems differed from each other. Some of the written languages focused on the relationship between spelling and pronunciation; some of them related the writing symbol more closely to the meaning. In general, there are three types of written systems: (1) phonetic system, as in the English alphabet; (2) syllabic system, as in Japanese syllabic script—kana; and (3) ideographic

汉字。中文书写系统是世界上唯一的至今仍在广泛使用的表意系统。由于表意文字的书写形式与语义相关，而语义总是十分复杂丰富的，所以表意的符号成千上万、千变万化，这也给书法家提供了发挥想象力和创造力的空间。

在中国，书法的兴盛时期可以追溯到几千年前。当人们开始书写的时候，也开始采用艺术的形式，试图写得美观，以满足各种需要。中国历史上出现了很多著名的书法家，他们不但创造了自己独具特色的书体，而且还通过书法作品展示了他们深厚的书法功力和内在的精神修养。随着科学技术的进步，比如造纸术和印刷术的发明，书法艺术得到了进一步的普及。事实上，中国书法的发展也反映了中国文明和文化的进程。

在中国，处处都可以看到书法作品，因为书法以其独特的社会功能融入了人们的生活之中。比如，中国人庆祝春节的时候，你在门柱上、墙上、屋子里或是贺年卡上，都可以看到写在红纸上的各种书法，以表示庆贺和祝福。人们也可以在宫殿、寺庙、亭台楼阁以及名山大川看到各具特色的书法作品（图7-1、图7-2、图7-3）。可以毫不夸张地说，中

system, as in Chinese characters. The Chinese writing system is the only ideographic system in the world that is still actively used. Since the writing form of ideographs is related to the meaning, and the meaning is always complicated, ideographic symbols are numerous and ever changing. It gives calligraphers space to use their imagination and creativity.

In China, the flourishing period of Chinese calligraphy can be traced back to thousands of years ago. When people began to write, they also began to write in an artistic style and write beautifully to meet various needs. There were many famous calligraphers in history who have created their own unique styles and demonstrated their skills and spirit through their calligraphic works. The progress of science and technology, such as the invention of papermaking and printing, has also provided the possibility for popularization of calligraphy. In fact, the development of Chinese calligraphy also mirrors the history of Chinese civilization and culture.

Since calligraphy has a unique social function that is closely linked to people's daily life, you can find calligraphic works everywhere in China. For example, when Chinese people celebrate the Spring Festival, calligraphic works can be seen on the gateposts, walls, inside of houses or on greeting cards. The characters are often written on red paper to express good wishes and hopes. Visitors can also see calligraphic works in palaces, temples, pavilions, towers,

国书法不仅是高雅的艺术，同时也是融入了大众生活的最流行的艺术之一。

中国书法起源于大自然。正如我们所看到的，不仅汉字的基础字形来源于自然，而且书法的基本规则也遵循了自然之美。如同高耸的山峰和奔流的江河，自然界变幻莫测的神韵融入了书法，而书法也反映出了大自然的勃勃生机。

图 7-1　泰山上的"五岳独尊"石刻
Figure 7-1　A stone with the inscriptions of "First of the Five Sacred Mountains" on Mount Tai

在中国，书法一直被认为是独具特色的最重要的艺术之一。书法、绘画与诗歌一起构成了辉煌灿烂的中国艺术。在古代中国，不精通书法的人难以通过朝廷为选拔官员而设立的科举考试。纵

famous mountains and rivers (Figure 7-1, 7-2 & 7-3). It is not exaggerated to say that Chinese calligraphy is not only an elegant art, but also one of the most popular arts which has merged into people's lives.

Chinese calligraphy derives from nature. As we can see, not only are the basic character forms derived from nature, but also that the principles of calligraphy are based on the beauty of nature. Like towering mountains and flowing rivers, the unpredictable charm of nature is integrated into calligraphy, and Chinese calligraphy reflects the vigor of nature.

In China, calligraphy has been considered one of the major arts with unique characteristics. Calligraphy, painting and poetry together constitute splendid Chinese art. In ancient China, it was impossible to pass the civic service examination for a government job if you were not proficient in calligraphy. Throughout the history of Chinese culture, outstanding scholars, painters, writers, or poets were often great calligraphers as well. In fact, many scholars and artists consider calligraphy as the door to art. Only by learning calligraphy can you enter the palace of art. As Mr. Chen Tingyou said, "Calligraphy is the painting without images, a piece of music without sounds, the dance without actors and actresses, and a building without components and materials".[1] In fact, various arts are related to and influence each other.

---

[1] Chen, Tingyou (2003) *Chinese Calligraphy*. Beijing: China Intercontinental Press.

观中国文化史，杰出的学者、画家、作家或诗人往往也都是书法高手。实际上，很多学者和艺术家都把书法看成是通往艺术之门的必由之路，只有习得书法，才可以进入艺术的宫殿。如陈廷祐先生所说："书法是没有物象的绘画，没有声音的音乐，没有演员的舞蹈，不用构件、材料的建筑。"[1] 其实，各种艺术都是相互关联、相互影响的。艺术的基本要素体现在平衡、变化、连贯、韵律等方面，这些正是书法艺术所强调的。书法综合了艺术所呈现的美的各种成分。

中国的儿童从小就开始练习书法。对孩子来说，画画儿和书法是培养他们审美意识的开始。对学习中文的外国学生来说，练习书法也大有帮助。中国汉字往往是中文学习过程中最大的障碍之一，而书法练习不仅可以增加学习者的学习兴趣和动力，而且也能使他们通过对字形结构和笔画笔顺的分析增强对汉字的记忆。通过练习书法，学生会更加欣赏中国语言的书写系统和造字方法，使学习汉字成为充满乐趣且难以忘却的经历。现代研究还证明，学习中国书法

---

[1] 陈廷祐（2003）《中国书法》，北京：五洲传播出版社。

The basic elements of art focus on balance, change, continuity, and rhythm, as does Chinese calligraphy. Calligraphy integrates these beautiful elements of art.

Children in China are encouraged to practice calligraphy at an early age. For children, painting and calligraphy are their first approach to aesthetic consciousness. It is also very helpful for foreign students to practice calligraphy while they are learning Chinese. Chinese characters are one of the hardest parts of the Chinese language for them to acquire. Calligraphic exercises can not only increase students' interest and motivation to learn, but also help them memorize the characters by analyzing the structure and strokes of each character. Through the practice of calligraphy, students will come to appreciate the Chinese writing system and the creation of Chinese characters, having an enjoyable and unforgettable experience in learning characters. Modern research has proved that learning Chinese calligraphy

图 7-2 故宫"正大光明"牌匾
Figure 7-2 *Zhengda Guangming* (meaning "frank and honest") inscribed on the plaque of the Imperial Palace

有益于人的大脑发展，因为书写汉字时不仅需要集中精神，保持安静，而且也需要人的左右脑同时活动起来，对每个汉字的音、形、义三方面进行综合考虑。比较而言，写英文的时候，人们只需考虑音和义两个方面。

中国有一句俗语："见字如见人。"这句话恰恰反映出中国人长期以来的观念，即从一纸书写中就可以窥见书写者的教育水平、社会地位和性格人品。因此我们也需要练习书法，并尽量把字写得更好更美。

英国美学家和艺术批评家里德（1893—1968）说："自从我们西方人熟悉中国文化以来，我们就知道中国人似乎超乎寻常地重视他们的书法。"的确，以汉字为载体的中国书法艺术是中华民族的文化瑰宝，是中国传统艺术和文化的核心。书法作为中国特有的传统艺术，在西方没有与之相对应的艺术形式。西方人学习中国书法时

can help with the development of the brain, since it involves both sides of the brain by simultaneously requiring concentration and calmness, while dealing with the sound, shape and meaning of each character. In comparison, when writing English, the brain is only involved with the sound and meaning of the word.

There is a common saying in China, "one's handwriting mirrors his face". This saying explains the belief held up by Chinese people—just a piece of calligraphic work reveals the writer's education level, social status, personal character and spirit. Therefore, we also need to practice calligraphy, and make our handwriting as good and beautiful as possible.

British aesthetician and art critic Herbert E. Read (1893–1968) said: "Since Westerners are getting familiar with Chinese culture, we know that the Chinese people have paid extraordinary attention to their calligraphy." Indeed, Chinese calligraphy, carried by Chinese characters, is the treasure of national culture, and is also the core of traditional Chinese art and culture. Calligraphy is a unique traditional art in China. There is no corresponding art form in the Western world.

图 7-3　北京颐和园长廊
Figure 7-3　The Long Corridor in the Summer Palace of Beijing

遭遇挑战也是在所难免的。

英国文化史家和批评家巴克森德尔（1933—2008）在其《意图的模式》一书中说："我向来歆慕中国，尤其是歆慕她的书法传统。这有几方面的原因，其中一个明显的原因便是：这个传统赋予了中国文化一种深刻的特质，我愿称之为一种介于人人都具备的言语与视觉文化之间的'中介语汇'。"多姿多彩的中国书法以其独特魅力令世人折服。书法艺术是中国的国粹。书法在东方艺术中表现了中国的特色，也是世界文化领域极其稀有的宝藏。书法的发展体现了中华民族的智慧和创造精神。

7.2 中国书法的源流

要想充分欣赏中国的书法艺术，就必须对中国书法的源流有所了解。中国的书法艺术是在汉字出现后才逐步发展起来的，但是，不论是汉字还是书法都起源于自然。离开了对自然的观察和欣赏，就不会有汉字和书法的存在。当汉字刚刚开始出现并初步定型后，人们首先要做的是简化和符号化这些图形文字。随后，历朝历代的书法家都根据自己对书法艺术的认识做出了自己独特的贡献，

Encountering challenges for Westerners to learn Chinese calligraphy is inevitable.

British art historian and critic Michael Baxandall (1933–2008) in his book *Patterns of Intention* said: "I have always admired China, especially her calligraphy tradition. There are several reasons, one of the obvious reasons is that tradition gives a profound trait of Chinese culture, and I would like to call it an intermediary between everyone's language and visual culture." The colorful Chinese calligraphy has impressed many people in the world by its unique charm. The calligraphy art is the national quintessence. Calligraphy demonstrates the Chinese characteristics in the Oriental art. It is also the world's rare cultural treasure. The development of calligraphy is filled with Chinese wisdom and creativity.

7.2 The Historical Origin of Chinese Calligraphy

It is important to understand the history of Chinese calligraphy in order to fully appreciate its visual beauty. The art of Chinese calligraphy developed along with the emergence of Chinese characters with both taking their origins from nature. There would have been no Chinese characters and calligraphy without observation and appreciation of nature. In the beginning, when the character forms were first standardized, the first thing people had to do was to simplify and symbolize these pictographic writings. Subsequently, in each succeeding dynasty, calligraphers made their own unique

他们的书法作品也得到了大众的认可。但是，无论是书法家还是一般民众，他们的审美意识都来自大自然，都受到大自然之美的启示，并由此形成了一个带有中国特色的悠久的文化传统。

中国人对书法独具特色的审美观是长期以来逐步形成的。在中国，书法和绘画有着密不可分的关系，两者都强调运笔用墨的熟练技巧，而这些技巧都需要由书法起步。所以，一个初学者在学习中国画之前，必须先学习和掌握书法的基础。总之，无论书法还是绘画，笔墨的运用挥洒都要反映出自然的和谐与韵律。元代（1206—1368）著名书法家、画家赵孟頫（1254—1322）十分重视书

contributions according to their understanding of the art of calligraphy and their works were recognized by the public. However, no matter calligraphers or common people, their aesthetic consciousness came from nature and was inspired by the beauty of nature. Through this, a long-standing tradition was born with Chinese characteristics.

Chinese people's unique aesthetic attitude towards calligraphy has gradually developed over a long period of time. In China, calligraphy and painting have an intimate relationship. Both calligraphy and painting stress the skills of manipulating the brush and ink, skills directly taken from calligraphy. Therefore, a beginner must learn and understand the fundamentals of calligraphy before learning painting. In a word, in either calligraphy or painting, the brush movement should reflect the harmony and rhythm of

图 7-4　元代赵孟頫《鹊华秋色图》（局部）
Figure 7-4　*A Painting of Autumn Scenery* (partial view) by Zhao Mengfu, Yuan Dynasty

法和绘画的共同源流（图 7-4）。在中国，这种审美流派被称为"文人画"，即中国文人画家和书法家在绘画和书法中更侧重于自我风格和气质的表达，而不是直观的外在形式。这种审美标准对书法和绘画都同样适用。

7.3 中国书法的历史

1. 甲骨文和殷商时期的书法

迄今为止，中国发现的最早期的书体是甲骨文（图 7-5）。从清朝末年发现甲骨文开始，目前已发掘出十几万片甲骨，辨认出大约 4500 个单字。所以，中国书法的源流可以追溯到殷商时期。这些单字的造型虽然与字义密不可分，但是笔画的组合、偏旁的位置及字形结构都体现出了艺术的构思。甲骨文的书刻者在汉字造型上表现出了非凡的艺术追求。甲骨文不仅是中国书法的开端，而且也为中国书法艺术的发展奠定了基础（图 7-6）。

2. 大篆和周朝时期的书法

大篆是在甲骨文的基础上发展起来的（图 7-7）。现存的大篆字体多见于周代刻铸于青铜器上的文字，称为"金文"，意即锲刻浇铸在金属上的文字。与

nature. Zhao Mengfu (1254–1322), a master of both calligraphy and painting in the Yuan Dynasty (1206–1368), stressed the common origin of the two arts (Figure 7-4). In China, this aesthetic school is called *Wenrenhua*, or "literati painting". It is the ideal of a Chinese scholar, painter and calligrapher to be more interested in individual expression and spirit than in immediate visual appeal on paper. This aesthetic attitude is applied to both calligraphy and painting.

7.3 The History of Chinese Calligraphy

1. Oracle bone inscriptions and calligraphy in the Shang Dynasty

Up to now, the earliest found examples of script were oracle bone inscriptions (Figure 7-5). Since the last years of the Qing Dynasty, more than one hundred thousand pieces of animal bones have been unearthed, and about 4,500 Chinese characters were identified. Thus, the origin of Chinese calligraphy can be traced back to the Shang Dynasty. Although the structures of these characters are inseparable from their corresponding meanings, the combination of the strokes, the position of the radicals and structures reflect artistic conceptions. The writers of oracle bone inscriptions demonstrated their extraordinary artistic pursuit in the structures of these Chinese characters. Oracle bone inscriptions are not only the beginning of Chinese calligraphy, but also the foundation for the development of Chinese calligraphy art (Figure 7-6).

图 7-5　商代刻在兽骨上的甲骨文
Figure 7-5　Oracle bone inscriptions inscribed on animal bones, Shang Dynasty

图 7-6　罗振玉（1866—1940）书写的甲骨文对联
Figure 7-6　Couplets written in the oracle bone inscriptions by Luo Zhenyu (1866–1940)

商代相比，西周的文化有了很大的进步，是上古文明的兴盛时期。金文反映了这个时期文化进步的一个侧面，同时也反映了当时社会对文字的重视。金文的书写艺术远远高于甲骨文，因为要在贵重的金属上刻铸文字，当然要求慎重而认真，所以多由当时的书法高手亲自书写。金文字体具有古典雅致的韵味，一直影响着后世的书法创作。

图 7-7　西周《大盂鼎》铭文，大篆
Figure 7-7　Inscriptions on *Dayu Ding* in the great seal style, Western Zhou Dynasty

2. The great seal style and calligraphy in the Zhou Dynasty

The great seal style develops on the basis of oracle bone inscriptions (Figure 7-7). Inscriptions cast on bronze vessels of the Zhou Dynasty are the surviving examples in the great seal style. These inscriptions are called *Jinwen*, meaning the script that is engraved on metal. Compared with that of the Shang Dynasty, the Western Zhou civilization had progressed much more. It was regarded as a prosperous period in ancient civilization. *Jinwen* shows us one aspect of such cultural progress and also reveals the emphasis that the society put upon writing. The art of writing *Jinwen* is much more advanced than that of oracle bone inscriptions because one must be cautious in order to write on precious metal. The writing was usually performed by experts of calligraphy. The style of *Jinwen* looks classic and

3. 小篆和秦代书法

秦始皇于公元前 221 年建立中央集权的秦朝以后，为了统一文字，按照易于辨认、易于书写、易于推行的原则，确定了小篆字体（图 7-8）。可以说，小篆的字体更加严整规范，结构也更趋于对称平衡。从大篆到小篆的变化体现了书法艺术的进步。

图 7-8　秦代李斯《峄山刻石》，小篆
Figure 7-8　*Yishan Ke Shi* (meaning "Inscriptions on the Stone of Mount Yi") in the small seal style by Li Si, Qin Dynasty

4. 隶书和汉代书法

在汉代 400 多年的历史中，各种书体的雏形和尝试也都陆续出现。然而，汉代书法艺术的代表还是隶书（图 7-9）。

elegant and has had great influence on the calligraphy of later periods.

3. The small seal style and calligraphy in the Qin Dynasty

After setting up the centralized government of the Qin Dynasty in 221 B.C., Emperor Qin Shihuang ordered the standardization of the writing system. Thus, the small seal style was established in order to clarify, simplify and promote writing (Figure 7-8). It could be said that the small seal style is neater, more standardized and more balanced in structure. The change from the great seal style to the small seal style reflects the progress of the art of calligraphy.

4. The clerical style and calligraphy in the Han Dynasty

During over 400 years of the Han Dynasty, embryonic forms of various styles and attempts of those styles emerged successively. However, the representative style of calligraphy in the Han Dynasty was the clerical style (Figure 7-9). Compared with the seal style, the clerical style increases the strokes of left falling and right falling, and is more flexible since it has no restrictions as to the uniformity of length or width of lines. The strokes are variable and lines are of different width. Horizontal with a rising tail and right falling with a broad ending, are often used to show the calligraphers' unrestrained spirit and characteristics. With more emphasis on the beginning and ending of strokes, the clerical style gains more room for creativity and development. Such a style looks both solemn

图7-9 东汉《熹平石经》，隶书
Figure 7-9 *Xiping Steles* in the clerical style, Eastern Han Dynasty

与篆书相比，隶书不仅增加了撇、捺等笔画，而且更加自由，不受线条长短一致、粗细一律等规则的束缚，笔画出现了很多变化，线条也粗细不匀，常用尾端上翘的横画和粗重的捺笔来展现书写者自由奔放的精神与豪放洒脱的性格。由于隶书更加注重笔画的起笔与收笔，在艺术上有了更大的发展空间，因而字体显得既庄重严肃又灵活多变，成为一种广泛使用的书体。

在汉代，造纸技术的发展对书法的普及和推广起到了十分积极的作用，除了隶书大兴之外，也出现了楷书、行书与草书的萌芽。

5. 楷书、行书、草书与唐代书法

唐代是中国历史上国力鼎盛的时期，商业经济的发达也促进了文化教育的发展。由于唐朝开国皇帝李世民（599—

and flexible, resulting in its widespread use.

In the Han Dynasty, the development of papermaking technology greatly facilitated the popularization and promotion of calligraphy. In addition to the popular clerical style, initial forms of the regular style, the running style and the grass style also began to emerge.

5. The regular style, the running style, the grass style and calligraphy in the Tang Dynasty

The Tang Dynasty was a period of great prosperity in China's history. The commercial development at that time boosted the development of culture and education. Since the first Tang emperor Li Shimin (599–649) and his successors loved calligraphy, especially Wang Xizhi's (303–361) calligraphy, the art of calligraphy was highly valued. Script forms such as the regular style, the running style and the grass style were also maturing, and have developed rapidly on the basis of the original embryonic forms, being collectively known as "modern script".

Even before the Tang Dynasty, there were many breakthroughs in calligraphy (Figure 7-10). Wang Xizhi (Figure 7-11), a master calligrapher from the Eastern Jin Dynasty (317–420), first learned from others then developed a school of his own (Figure 7-12). His calligraphy has had such far-reaching influence that he has been honored as a "saint calligrapher". Wang Xianzhi (344–386), the seventh son of Wang Xizhi, inherited his father's style and made further changes to traditional calligraphy (Figure 7-13). Wang

649）及他的继承者都酷爱书法，尤其是对王羲之（303—361）的书法十分推崇，所以书法艺术受到了高度重视。楷书、行书和草书等书体也日趋成熟，在原有雏形的基础上得到了迅猛发展，当时称为"现代书体"。

在唐代之前，中国就已经出现了很多书法的创新（图7-10）。王羲之（图7-11）是东晋（317—420）时期的大书法家，他的书法艺术博采众长，推陈出新（图7-12），因而独树一帜，影响十分深远，被后世尊称为"书圣"。他的第七子王献之（344—386）在继承父亲风格的基础上，进一步改变了传统的书风（图7-13），父子二人并称为"二王"。

由于书法艺术在唐代受到广泛的重视，深受大众喜爱，因而出现了不少卓

Xizhi and Wang Xianzhi are together known as the "two Wangs".

Since the art of calligraphy was highly regarded and enjoyed great popularity during the Tang Dynasty, there arose many distinguished calligraphers. The regular style, the most standard and popular style continues to be used today. Six noted masters in the regular style of this dynasty were Ou

图 7-10 《王建哀册》是五代（907—960）楷书的代表
Figure 7-10 *Mourning for Wang Jian*, masterpiece of the regular style, Five Dynasties (907–960)

(Ouyang Xun, 557–641) (Figure 7-14), Yu (Yu Shinan, 558–638), Chu (Chu Suiliang, 596–659) (Figure 7-15), Xue (Xue Ji, 649–713), Yan (Yan Zhenqing, 709–784) (Figure 7-16) and Liu (Liu Gongquan, 778–865) (Figure 7-17). All the six masters held their brush in stringent control and their characters

图 7-11 王羲之像
Figure 7-11 The portrait of Wang Xizhi

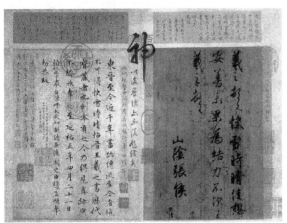

图 7-12　东晋王羲之《快雪时晴帖》
Figure 7-12　*Kuai Xue Shi Qing Tie* (meaning "Book of Model Calligraphy on a Clear Day after Brief Snow") by Wang Xizhi, Eastern Jin Dynasty

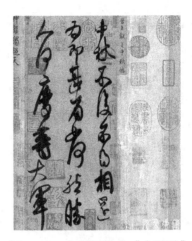

图 7-13　东晋王献之《中秋贴》
Figure 7-13　*Book of Model Calligraphy on the Mid-Autumn Festival* by Wang Xianzhi, Eastern Jin Dynasty

有成就的大书法家。楷书成为最规范也最受欢迎的书体，流传至今。在唐代，最擅长楷书的有书法"六大家"——欧（欧阳询，557—641）（图7-14）、虞（虞世南，558—638）、褚（褚遂良，596—659）（图7-15）、薛（薛稷，649—713）、颜（颜真卿，709—784）

were extremely coherent and tight in form. Among these styles, the most widely spread and influential are the Yan style and the Liu style. The simple and vigorous Yan style and the firm and elegant Liu style have become models for later generations of calligraphy. In a word, the art of calligraphy in the Tang Dynasty constitutes a glorious chapter in the history of Chinese calligraphy.

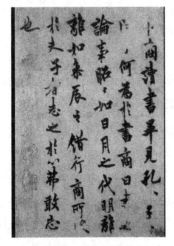

图 7-14　唐代欧阳询《卜商帖》
Figure 7-14　*Bu Shang Tie* (meaning "Book of Model Calligraphy on Business Divination") by Ouyang Xun, Tang Dynasty

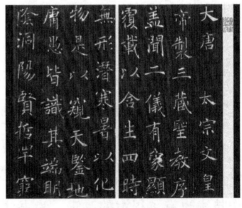

图 7-15　唐代褚遂良《雁塔圣教序》
Figure 7-15　*Yanta Shengjiao Xu* (meaning "Preface of Holy Doctrine Erected before the Wild Goose Tower") by Chu Suiliang, Tang Dynasty

（图7-16）、柳（柳公权，778—865）
（图7-17）。他们书法的共同特点是运笔流畅有力，字形结构严谨，风格连贯统一。其中，流传最广、影响最大的为颜体和柳体。颜体浑厚刚健，柳体坚挺秀丽，成为后世书法的楷模。总之，唐代书法艺术在中国书法史上写下了辉煌的篇章。

6. The development of calligraphy in the Song Dynasty

The art of calligraphy was at its peak in the Tang Dynasty. During the Song Dynasty (960–1279), the civil service examination system was perfected and calligraphy was inevitably given due attention. At the same time, the Song Dynasty saw a large improvement in the production of the "four treasures" in the writing studio (brush,

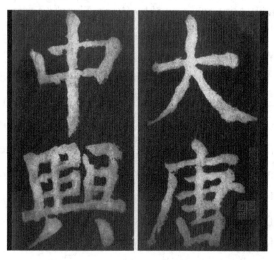

图 7-16　唐代颜真卿《中兴颂》
Figure 7-16　*Ode to the Resurgence* by Yan Zhenqing, Tang Dynasty

图 7-17　唐代柳公权《玄秘塔碑》
Figure 7-17　*Xuanmi Tower Stele* by Liu Gongquan, Tang Dynasty

6. 宋代书法艺术的发展

书法艺术在唐代达到极盛，到了宋代（960—1279），随着科举考试制度的进一步完善，重视书法艺术已经成为一种必然的趋势。与此同时，文房四宝的制作技术也有了很大的改进，为书法艺术的普及与提高创造了更好的条件。此外，在宋代庆历年间（1041—1048），

ink stick, paper and ink stone), which promoted the prevalence and development of calligraphy. During the Qingli period (1041–1048) of the Song Dynasty, Mr. Bi Sheng (972–1051) invented the clay movable type printing, which made the printing of books more convenient (Figure 7-18). So, a large number of writing scripts were copied in this dynasty, helping promote and popularize traditional Chinese calligraphy.

毕昇（972—1051）首创了泥活字版印刷术，使图书印刷更为方便（图 7-18）。因此，宋代大量刻印书帖，使中国传统的书法艺术得到了推广和普及。值得一提的是，宋朝的皇帝大多治国无术，但都迷恋书法，其中尤以宋徽宗赵佶（1082—1135）为代表。他在政治上昏庸无能，但是在书法艺术上却精益求精，独创"瘦金体"（图 7-19），流传至今。

图 7-18　泥活字版
Figure 7-18　Clay movable type board

7. 清代的书法艺术

清代是中国历史上最后一个封建王朝，中国书画艺术在这个时期也进入了集大成的高峰时期。清代帝王，尤其是康熙（1654—1722）（图 7-20）、乾隆（1711—1799），不仅都是书法家，而且都大力提倡书法，为书法艺术的发展创造了良好的环境。乾隆皇帝十分推崇元代书法家赵孟頫，搜集了很多他的作

Something worth mentioning is the fact that most emperors of the Song Dynasty were infatuated with calligraphy, and yet they proved incompetent in managing state affairs.

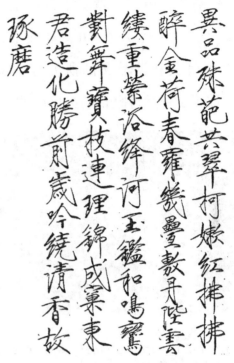

图 7-19　宋徽宗赵佶瘦金体诗抄
Figure 7-19　A poem in the slender gold style by Zhao Ji, Emperor Huizong of the Song Dynasty

A case in point is Zhao Ji (1082–1135), Emperor Huizong of the Song Dynasty, who was inept in politics but kept improving his calligraphy until he created the "slender gold style" (Figure 7-19). His influential works in this area are still highly regarded today.

7. Calligraphy in the Qing Dynasty

The last feudal dynasty in Chinese history, the Qing Dynasty, witnessed a collective prosperity in calligraphy and painting. Emperors of the Qing Dynasty, especially Kangxi (1654–1722) (Figure 7-20)

品，使赵体在颜体、柳体的基础上得到了推广。赵体柔中有刚，灵活生动，存世书迹较多，深受大众喜爱（图7-21）。

在清代，由于大量青铜器出土，甲骨文、钟鼎文被发现，并刻印成书，所以对甲骨文和钟鼎文的研究也兴盛起来，取得了令后世瞩目的突出成就。

and Qianlong (1711–1799), were not only calligraphers themselves, but also advocated calligraphy, creating a favorable environment for its development. Emperor Qianlong was an avid collector of the works of Zhao Mengfu from the Yuan Dynasty. His admiration of Zhao enhanced the influence and prevalence of the Zhao style along with the Yan and Liu styles. Characterized by vigor, grace, flexibility and liveliness, the Zhao style is well-preserved in many surviving works and is still popular today (Figure 7-21).

With the unearthing of many bronze vessels in the Qing Dynasty, oracle bone inscriptions and the bronze inscriptions were discovered and many rubbings were made based on those inscriptions. So, the study of oracle bone inscriptions and bronze inscriptions flourished, making outstanding achievements that attract the attention of later generations.

图 7-20 康熙题 "避暑山庄"
Figure 7-20 *Bishu Shanzhuang* (meaning "mountain resort") inscribed by Emperor Kangxi, Qing Dynasty

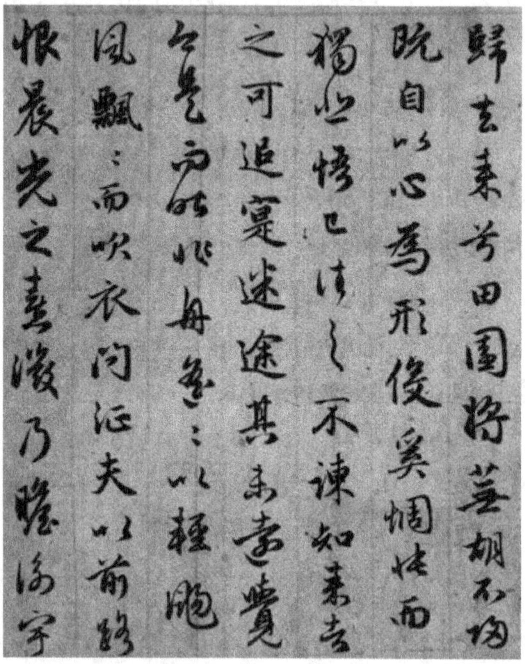

图 7-21 元代赵孟頫《归去来辞》，行书
Figure 7-21 *Guiqulai Ci* (meaning "A Ballad for My Coming Back") in the running style by Zhao Mengfu, Yuan Dynasty

思考题 **Questions**

1. 什么是"书法"？

2. 世界上有多少种主要的书写系统？汉字属于哪种书写系统？

3. 为什么说汉字为书法家提供了发挥想象力和创造力的空间？

4. 中国书法的历史有多长？

5. 中国书法发展的根源是什么？

6. 中国书法在东方艺术中占有什么样的地位？

7. 为什么要学习中国书法？

8. 为什么中国书法和绘画有着密不可分的联系？

9. 中国文人书法家的审美观是什么？

1. What is calligraphy?

2. How many types of writing systems are there in the world? Which writing system do Chinese characters belong to?

3. Why do Chinese characters provide space for calligraphers to use their imagination and creativity?

4. How long is the history of Chinese calligraphy?

5. What is the basic inspiration of Chinese calligraphy?

6. What is the status of Chinese calligraphy in Oriental art?

7. Why do we learn Chinese calligraphy?

8. Why does Chinese calligraphy have an intimate relationship with painting?

9. What is the Chinese literati calligraphers' aesthetic attitude towards calligraphy?

第八章　文房四宝

Chapter Eight　The "Four Treasures" of the Writing Studio

中国书法和绘画独具特色的发展与所使用的工具是密不可分的。这些工具的使用直接影响到书法与绘画的表现形式。所谓"文房四宝"，指的就是中国书法中使用的书写工具——笔、墨、纸、砚（图8-1、图8-2）。"文房四宝"是书

The unique development of Chinese calligraphy and painting is inseparable from the writing tools. The use of these tools have directly influenced the forms that calligraphy and painting have taken. The concept of the "four treasures" of the writing studio refers to the tools used in Chinese writing—brush, ink stick, paper, and ink stone (Figure 8-1 & 8-2). The "four treasures" of the writing studio are indispensable in calligraphy practice. As the ancient Chinese said, "You must first sharpen your tools if you want to do a good job." If you want to do a good job, you must have tools ready. This is true in the practice of calligraphy. You can't write well without a good set of the "four treasures" in your writing studio.

图 8-1　文房四宝
Figure 8-1　The "four treasures" of the writing studio

法练习中必不可少的。古人说："工欲善其事，必先利其器。"要想做好一件事，必须先准备好工具。书法练习也是一样。选不好"文房四宝"，就写不出好字来。

8.1 笔

笔是书法练习中最重要的工具。传统的书法主要使用的是毛笔（图8-3）。毛笔

图 8-2　文房四宝
Figure 8-2　The "four treasures" of the writing studio

图 8-3　各种毛笔
Figure 8-3　All kinds of brushes

的使用历史可以追溯到商朝。制作毛笔的基本材料是竹管、木管和动物的毛发。随着时间的推移，毛笔的制作也不断改良，其外形越来越精美，笔杆有时选用金、银、玉、象牙、龟甲等贵重材料制作，即使制作普通毛笔也会考虑外形的美观。除此之外，笔托、笔架（图 8-4）、笔筒（图 8-5）等都与书法的审美要求相关，而且增添了书法练习中的美感。

图 8-4　笔架
Figure 8-4　Brush rack

图 8-5　清代乾隆年间的笔筒
Figure 8-5　Brush holder made in the reign of Qianlong of Qing Dynasty

一支毛笔最重要的是笔锋。笔锋质量的不断提高，给书法家提供了越来越

8.1 Brush

The brush is the most important tool in the practice of calligraphy. Calligraphers mainly use the brush (Figure 8-3) for traditional Chinese calligraphic works. The use of brushes can be traced back to the Shang Dynasty. The basic materials that make up a brush are bamboo, wood and animal hair. As time progressed, so did the brush. Brushes became quite elaborate in decoration, with valued materials such as gold, silver, jade, ivory, and tortoise shell to make brush holders. Even the common brush is made with aesthetic appeal in mind. In addition, the brush rest, brush rack (Figure 8-4) and brush holder (Figure 8-5) are all related to the aesthetic requirements of calligraphy, and add to the aesthetics of calligraphy.

The most important part of a brush is its tip. The development of the brush tip has provided the possibility for

大的发挥艺术才能的空间。毛笔的毛通常选用羊毛、兔毛、狼毛或貂毛。用羊毛或兔毛制成的毛笔写出来的字比较柔和、雅致，通常用来写行书或草书；用狼毛或貂毛制成的笔比较有弹性，适合写有力度的字；如果把羊毛和狼毛混合起来，就制成了兼毫笔，写出来的字具有刚柔相济的特点。毛笔根据不同的需要和审美的要求而制作，可以用来画画儿、着色，也可以用来书写广告或条幅。古人说："笔有四德：尖、齐、圆、健。"意思是，好的毛笔具有四个优点，陈廷祐先生对此进行了详细的解释："一是尖，能表现出笔画的精微变化；二是齐，笔毫散开时前端平齐，可使笔锋在纸上铺开，写出饱满有力的墨迹；三是圆，笔毫经常保持长长的圆锥状，便于向各个方向用力，如意地接触纸面；四是健，耐用并能保持弹性和柔韧性。使用毛笔，书法的作者可以写出具有不同体态、力度、弹性、节奏、气势的字。"[1]

毛笔是一个艺术家心灵的延伸，是其生命的一部分，艺术家通过笔锋的运转来表达他想要表达的一切。

---

[1] 陈廷祐（2003）《中国书法》，北京：五洲传播出版社。

calligraphers to bring their artistic talent into full play. Brushes are usually made of the hair of sheep, rabbit, wolf or sable. Sheep or rabbit hair brushes produce soft, graceful strokes and are usually used for the running or grass style. Wolf or sable hair brushes have greater elasticity and are suitable for writing powerful characters. If the tip of a brush consists of both sheep and wolf hair, the mixed hair produces blended tips. The written characters are characterized by a balance of hardness and softness. Brushes are designed according to different needs and aesthetic requirements. They can be used for painting, coloring, as well as for writing posters and banners. The ancients said: "the tip of a brush has four good points: pointed, even, round and tenacious". This means that a good brush has four advantages. As Mr. Chen Tingyou explains, "First, the tip of a brush could display the delicate changes of strokes. Second, its smooth end hair could make writing vigorous while it spread across the paper. Third, its cone shape made it easy to move in all directions. Fourth, it was durable, and kept its elasticity and softness longer. With such a brush, the calligrapher could write characters in different shapes, displaying different intensities and rhythms."[1]

The brush is an extension of an artist's heart, a part of the artist' life, who expresses everything through the tip of a brush.

In modern society, since a pen or a pencil

---

[1] Chen, Tingyou (2003) *Chinese Calligraphy*. Beijing: China Intercontinental Press.

在现代社会，由于钢笔或铅笔使用起来更方便，因而也更加普及。作为初学者，开始阶段使用钢笔、圆珠笔或铅笔来练习书法会更加实用、有效。事实上，硬笔书法越来越方便实用，也越来越大众化。

8.2 墨

笔和墨像一对孪生姐妹，形影不离，成为书法艺术家生命中不可分割的一部分。

传统上，中国书法所用的墨汁是用墨条在砚台上研磨而成的。墨的使用可以追溯到5000多年以前。在西安半坡村出土的陶器上可以看到，中国古人从那时起就开始使用炭墨了。到了汉代，墨的使用更加普遍，民间每个月都要向皇帝进贡墨。后来，墨成为每年必需的贡品之一。

墨是把干松炭、煤烟、桐油和胶等混合起来制成墨坯后干燥而成的。墨的制作由民间摸索逐渐成为一项专门的工艺。根据各自的要求，人们在市场上可以买到大小不同、形状

is more convenient to use, it is more popular. As beginners, it is more practical and efficient to practice calligraphy by using a pen, a ball-point pen or a pencil at the beginning. In fact, hard-tip calligraphy is getting more and more practical and popular.

8.2 Ink Stick

Brush and ink stick are looked upon as twins. They always work together. They are valued greatly as an integral part of a calligrapher's life.

Traditionally, the ink used for Chinese calligraphy is produced by an ink stick moistened with a little water and ground against an ink stone. The use of the ink stick can be traced back to 5,000 years ago. The pottery unearthed at Banpo Village, Xi'an, has shown that the ancient Chinese people started to use charcoal ink from that time on. The use of ink sticks became so widespread that during the Han Dynasty, the emperor ordered a monthly ink stick tribute, later to become an annual tribute.

Ink stick making is to mix dry pinewood charcoal, soot and tung oil with a binding agent, then allowing it to dry in a mold. Gradually, making ink sticks became a profession. Ink sticks now come in various shapes, sizes and colors which people can purchase at the markets

图 8-6　人物造型的墨
Figure 8-6 Ink sticks that resemble a man

图 8-7 十二生肖墨
Figure 8-7 Ink sticks that resemble the twelve Chinese zodiac animals

图 8-8 徽墨
Figure 8-8 The *Hui* ink sticks

图 8-9 五彩墨
Figure 8-9 Multicolored ink sticks

各异、颜色丰富的墨（图 8-6 至图 8-9）。墨条或墨块上还有描金字和各种图案作为装饰。一块好墨应该"黑为漆，硬为石"。如曲磊磊所说："墨的作用不可低估，因为一幅艺术作品要通过墨色才能体现出来。俗话说，黄金易得，好墨难求。"[1] 用好墨研磨出来的墨汁写成的书法作品可以保存很久而墨色不褪。现在我们仍能看到很多传世的书法作品，虽然年代久远，但是墨色如初。

现在人们写毛笔字时，为了方便和节省时间，往往使用墨汁。墨汁倒出来就可以使用，不需要自己用墨和砚台去研磨，自然是又省事又干净。但是许多书法爱好者仍然喜欢自己研磨墨汁（图 8-10），因为自己研磨的墨汁可以根据需要使浓淡更加得当；同时，磨墨本身也是一个宁神静气的过程，书写者可以一

according to their various needs (Figure 8-6 to 8-9). The ink stick may also be decorated with gold inscriptions and various pictures. A good quality ink stick should be as black as black paint and as solid as a stone. As Qu said, "Ink is treated very seriously since it is the means by which a work of art is manifested. There is a saying that it is easier to obtain gold than ink!"[1] The color of characters couldn't fade away if the ink is produced from a good ink stick. Many excellent calligraphic works created many years ago still show their color as bright as when first created.

For convenience and time saving, people nowadays often use manufactured ink to practice calligraphy. It is certainly convenient and neat to use ink directly from a bottle rather than grind the ink against an ink stone. However, many calligraphy lovers still prefer to grind ink by themselves (Figure 8-10), since they can create the desired ink consistency according to their needs. At the same time, the process of grinding ink gently against the ink stone gives them concentration and inspiration, allowing the calligraphers to

---

[1] 曲磊磊（2002）《中国书法艺术简论》。英国：奇科什图书。

[1] Qu, Lei Lei (2002) *The Simple Art of Chinese Calligraphy*. Great Britain: Cico Books.

边磨墨一边进行书法作品的构思，这也是一种乐趣。难怪有些书法家认为，学习书法必须先学磨墨。

图 8-10　研磨墨汁
Figure 8-10　Grinding ink against the ink stone

8.3 纸

纸是中国古代"四大发明"之一。根据《后汉书》记载，纸的发明者是东汉（25—220）的蔡伦（61—121）（图 8-11）。从出土的文物来看，其实早在西汉（前 206—公元 25）时期，中国就有由麻质纤维制成的纸了。蔡伦总结前人的经验，改进造纸术，采用树皮、麻头、破布、渔网等原料，在公元 105 年造出

图 8-11　蔡伦像
Figure 8-11　The portrait of Cai Lun

work out the composition of a calligraphic work. It also brings them much pleasure. No wonder some calligraphers think that learning how to grind ink before learning how to write.

8.3 Paper

Paper is one of China's "four great inventions". According to the *History of the Later Han*, paper was invented by Cai Lun (61–121) (Figure 8-11) in the Eastern Han Dynasty (25–220). However, based on unearthed artifacts, China had paper made of hemp fiber as early as the Western Han Dynasty (206 B.C.–25 A.D.). Cai Lun combined the techniques of the predecessors, improved the technology of papermaking, and used tree bark, hemp, rags and fishing nets as raw materials to finally produce "Cai Lun Paper" in 105 A.D. The invention of paper replaced the silk (Figure 8-12) and bamboo (Figure 8-13) which had been used as the "paper" before. Silk was too expensive and the bulk of bamboo was too heavy. The emergence of paper promoted the further development of Chinese calligraphy.

As Chinese society developed, so did the variety of paper produced in China. In general, paper could be divided into two categories based on the materials of manufacture: rough or fine quality. The raw materials that were used to make paper

了"蔡伦纸"。纸的发明改写了古代书契用缣帛（图8-12）或竹简（图8-13）书写的历史。缣帛太贵，而竹简又太过笨重，纸的出现促进了中国书法的进一步发展。

图 8-12　汉代帛书《黄帝书》
Figure 8-12　*Huangdi Shu* (meaning "The Yellow Emperor's Four Canons") written in silk manuscripts, Han Dynasty

随着社会的发展，纸的种类也越来越多，一般有质料粗劣和精细的区别。造纸的原料包括稻麦的外壳、做丝绸的蚕茧，以及苔藓等，因产区的不同而有所不同。用于书法的纸张也有质料、大小和吸墨性等方面的不同。

在各种纸张中，最适合中国书法和绘画的是宣纸（图8-14）。宣纸的原产地主要是安徽宣城一带，所以得名"宣纸"。这种纸以青檀木的树皮及沙田稻

depended on the regional resources and included wheat or rice husks, silk cocoons, and mosses. Paper for calligraphy could vary in texture, size and absorption of ink.

图 8-13　武威汉简
Figure 8-13　Bamboo slips excavated in Wuwei

The most suitable paper for Chinese calligraphy and painting is *Xuan* paper (Figure 8-14). *Xuan* paper was originally produced in the region of Xuancheng, Anhui Province, so it has always been called "*Xuan* paper". This paper is made of green sandalwood bark and straw. Not only does *Xuan* paper have strong absorption on the surface, but it is also white, soft, vigorous, and resistant to color fading. It has been the best choice for Chinese calligraphers and painters for more than 1,000 years.

For beginners, it is better to use rough and inexpensive paper to practice calligraphy. A new kind of paper has been invented now that can be used again and again to practice calligraphy, which is certainly good news for beginners of calligraphy.

图 8-14　工人在制作宣纸
Figure 8-14　A worker is making *Xuan* paper.

草等为原料，不仅吸水性强，而且质地白、柔软、拉力大，久藏不会变色，因此 1000 多年以来，它一直是书法和绘画用纸的最佳选择。

对于初学者来说，最好选用质料相对粗劣而且价格比较便宜的纸来练习。现在，又出现了可以反复使用的书法练习用纸，这无疑是初学者的福音。

8.4 砚

砚台的作用是通过墨的研磨而产生墨汁，用于书法或绘画。它也是书法练习中的重要工具之一。用来制作砚台的材料很多，比如石头、陶瓦、玉器、铜器等，但是最常用的还是石头（图8-15）。据说，做砚台最好的石材出自大山深处的石洞。好的砚台摸起来有潮湿感且表面坚硬，不会因墨汁的浸泡而发

8.4 Ink Stone

The function of an ink stone is to grind the solid ink stick into a usable liquid for calligraphy and painting. It is also one of the vital tools for the practice of calligraphy. There are various materials used to make ink stones, such as stone, terracotta, jade, copper and so on; however, stone is still the most common (Figure 8-15). The best stones are said to come from caves deep inside mountains. An ink stone is considered good if it is moist to the touch and has a hard surface which takes the ink well without sticking. A good ink stone must also be solid, smooth and produce ink quickly without damaging the brush. Stones like these are found in the provinces of Anhui, Guangdong, Shandong and Gansu. It is said that the best known are *Duan* ink stones from Guangdong. In general, there are three different levels of quality with stones found in the deepest levels of a cave being considered the best. Because they were located in the heart of the mountain and were constantly soaked by underground steam, these stones have the moistness, and they

图 8-15　各种砚台
Figure 8-15　All kinds of ink stones

黏变软。砚台的表面不但要硬，而且要光滑，生墨快且不会损害毛笔。这样的石头出自安徽、广东、山东和甘肃等地，据说广东的端砚最好。一般来说，制作砚台的石材分为三级。最好的在最底层，因为它们位于山峰的中心地带，不断受到地气的浸润，所以石头带有天然的潮湿，非常适合制作砚台。由于历朝历代连续不断的挖掘开采，现在已经越来越难找到好的石材了。

很多砚台本身就是一件艺术品，有的砚台顶端或四周带有各种雕刻。很多艺术家把砚台作为他们忠实的好伙伴。

were found to be quite suitable for ink stones. Due to succeeding dynasties mining for the stones, it became more and more difficult to find stones of high quality.

Many ink stones themselves can be considered works of art; some ink stones have various carvings on the top or around them. Many artists consider their ink stones their good friends who remain loyal for a lifetime.

思考题 Questions

1. 中国书法和书写工具有什么关系？
2. "文房四宝" 是什么意思？
3. "文房四宝" 包括什么？
4. 你同意中国古人说的 "工欲善其事，必先利其器" 吗？请举例说明。
5. 练习书法最重要的书写工具是什么？
6. 毛笔最重要的部分是什么？应该怎

1. What is the relationship between Chinese calligraphy and writing tools?
2. What does the concept of the "four treasures" of the writing studio refer to?
3. What are the "four treasures" of the writing studio?
4. Do you agree with the ancient Chinese saying that "You must first sharpen your tools if you want to do a good job"? Please give an example.

样选择毛笔？

7. 中国人是什么时候开始使用墨的？

8. 为什么很多书法家仍然喜欢自己磨墨而不是用现成的墨汁？

9. 纸是中国古代"四大发明"之一，最适合中国书法的是什么纸？为什么？

10. 砚台的作用是什么？

5. What is the most important writing tool in the practice of Chinese calligraphy?

6. What is the most important part of a brush? How to choose a brush?

7. When did Chinese people start to use the ink stick?

8. Why do many calligraphers still prefer to grind ink by themselves rather than use manufactured ink?

9. Paper is one of China's "four great inventions". What kind of paper is most suitable for Chinese calligraphy? Why?

10. What is the function of an ink stone?

第九章 "永"字八法

Chapter Nine The Eight Basic Strokes of Character *Yong*

9.1 什么是"永"字八法？

尽管汉字数以万计，由各种笔画组成，但是中国古代的书法家通过长期的艺术创作实践，将所有的笔画归纳为八种，并且通过一个汉字体现出来。这个汉字念 yǒng，意思是"永久"。"永"字所代表的八种笔画被称为"永"字八法（图 9-1）。长久以来，人们就以"永"字八法为基础来练习各种笔画，这也成为楷书入门的基本功。虽然"永"字并不能包括汉字的所有笔画，但是掌握它的八个笔画就能书写或简单或复杂的各种汉字。在中国，学习书法的学生常常会花费好几个月的时间来练习一种笔画。通过持续的练习，每个初学者都能收到成效。汉字的一点一画就像盖房子的一砖一瓦，没有这些材料，就不能盖房子；材料不符合要求，盖出来的房子就会东倒西歪。

图 9-1 "永"字八法
Figure 9-1 The eight basic strokes of character *Yong*

9.1 What Is the Eight Basic Strokes of Character *Yong*?

Although there are tens of thousands of Chinese characters, made up of many different strokes, calligraphers in Chinese history through long-term practice of artistic creation reduced all these strokes to eight basic strokes contained within one Chinese character. The eight basic strokes represented by the character "永", pronounced *yǒng* (meaning "forever"), are also known as the eight basic strokes of character *Yong* (Figure 9-1). Since ancient times, the eight basic strokes of character *Yong* have been used as an example for students to practice strokes. This has become the basic training for students who want to master the regular style. The character *Yong* does not include every stroke used to form all Chinese characters, but mastering its eight strokes will allow you to write characters from simple to complex. Calligraphy students in China often spend several months practicing a single stroke. Every beginner can produce very impressive results with continuous practice. Each dot or

所以，掌握汉字笔画的书写方法是学习中国书法的基础。

这八种笔画分别为：

1. 点

2. 横

3. 竖

4. 钩

5. 提

6. 撇

7. 短撇

8. 捺

要注意的是，上述八种笔画都有变体，而具体是哪种变体则取决于该笔画在每个汉字中的具体位置，所以练习"永"字八法要懂得举一反三，融会贯通。有人把笔画比作拼写文字的字母，因为字母组合在一起形成单词，而笔画组合在一起成为汉字。学习写汉字，要先从基本笔画的学习开始。用毛笔写字，笔锋的运用十分重要，运笔有"藏锋""露锋""中锋""侧锋"等分别。"藏锋"指不露笔锋，笔尖先向反方向运行；"露锋"指显露下笔时的笔锋；"中锋"指毛笔运行时，笔锋在笔画的中间；"侧锋"指运笔时，笔锋偏左或偏右。

stroke in a character is like a piece of brick or tile in a house. A house can't be built without building materials, and it won't be firm and steady if the materials don't meet the standard. So, mastering the writing method of strokes provides an essential grounding for learning Chinese calligraphy.

The eight strokes are listed as follows:

1. Dot

2. Horizontal

3. Vertical

4. Hook

5. Raise

6. Left falling

7. Aside

8. Right falling

Note that each of the above eight strokes has variations depending on its placement within the character. Therefore, to practice the eight basic strokes of character *Yong*, it is best to learn by analogy. It is suggested by some that the function of the strokes can be compared to the letters in an alphabetical language; letters are combined to form words whereas strokes are combined to form Chinese characters. Learning to write Chinese characters should begin with the practice of basic strokes. When writing with a brush, tip usage is significant. Tip usage can be differentiated between "hiding the tip", "revealing the tip", "mid tip" and "tip side". "Hiding the tip" refers to concealing the tip by moving the tip in an opposing direction; "revealing the tip" refers to exposing the tip in writing. "Mid tip" means the tip is in the

9.2 八个基本笔画的写法

下面介绍一下这八个基本笔画的写法。

1. 点

在中国传统书法中，"点"也称为"侧"。人们常说，"点"好像是一个字的眼睛。写"点"时，毛笔顺时针移动，形成一个比较柔和的三角形。书写方法是：（1）用毛笔笔锋向上挑；（2）转用中锋；（3）向右下方移动；（4）按笔；（5）提笔，用笔锋完成"点"的书写。

middle of the stroke when the brush is being moved; "tip side" refers to the left or to the right slant of the tip when writing.

9.2 The Writing Methods of the Eight Basic Strokes

The writing methods of the eight basic strokes are introduced as follows.

1. The dot

In traditional Chinese calligraphy, the dot was also called *Ce*. The dot is often said to be like the eye of a character. It is created by moving the brush in a clockwise circle, making a soft, triangular form. To make this stroke, (1) move the tip of a brush upward; (2) use the mid tip; (3) move downward to the right; (4) press downward; and (5) complete the dot by lifting the tip of a brush upward.

◆ 请参照下面的图示，按照毛笔的运笔步骤练习，并练习各种变体。

◇ Please refer to the examples below, follow the brush movement, and practice the variations.

2. 横

书写"横"画的方法是：（1）用毛笔笔锋轻按在纸上；（2）往下按笔，但毛笔并不移动；（3）用中锋向右移；（4）笔锋行至"横"画的尾部；（5）提笔锋，然后向右按笔；（6）用笔锋向反方向提笔。

2. The horizontal

To create the horizontal stroke, (1) press lightly the tip of a brush onto the paper; (2) press down briefly without moving the brush from the paper; (3) move the mid tip to the right; (4) reach the end of the horizontal stroke; (5) lift the tip upward, press the brush down to the right; and (6) finish by lifting the tip of a brush and moving backward.

◇ 请参照下面的图示，按照毛笔的运笔步骤练习，并练习各种变体。

◇ Please refer to the examples below, follow the brush movement, and practice the variations.

3. 竖

　　书写"竖"画的方法是：（1）用毛笔笔锋向上移；（2）停顿一下，转笔锋向下，按笔；（3）轻提笔，用毛笔中锋向下移；（4）在竖画尾部顿笔；（5）提笔，用毛笔笔锋沿"竖"画反向运笔，收笔处应圆润而有力度。

3. The vertical

　　To create the vertical stroke, (1) move the tip of a brush upward; (2) pause for a moment, then turn the tip and press down; (3) lift the tip and pull the mid tip downward; (4) pause at the end of the vertical stroke; and (5) pull the tip a little way back, retracing the line for a neat finish.

◇ 请参照下面的图示，按照毛笔的运笔步骤练习，并练习各种变体。

◇ Please refer to the example below, follow the brush movement, and practice the variations.

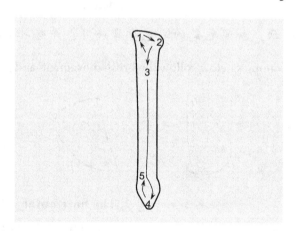

　　除了这种圆尾的"竖"之外，还有一种尖尾的"竖"，形状如下：

　　Besides the vertical stroke with a round tail, there is another kind of vertical stroke that has a sharp tail (see the example below).

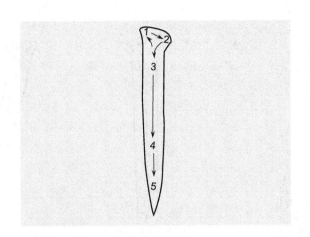

写尖尾"竖"时，只需要按照步骤（1）—（3）去写就行。但是，在第（3）步后要慢慢提笔，以求取得尖尾的效果。

4. 钩

"钩"画本身不是独立的笔画，一般与"横"画和"竖"画相连。钩的长短大小要跟与它相连的笔画相协调。写"钩"时，毛笔先按照写"竖"或"横"画的步骤（1）—（3）运笔，后面的步骤是：（4）提笔；（5）按笔；（6）提笔转锋；（7）慢慢提笔直到笔锋离开纸面，留下一个钩的形状。

When you write this kind of vertical, you only need to follow steps (1)-(3). But after step (3), you should lift the tip of a brush gradually, so as to finish with a sharp tail.

4. The hook

The hook stroke doesn't exist by itself. It has to connect with either the horizontal stroke or the vertical stroke. The hook stroke can be written in various ways depending on the strokes it connects with. For the hook, (1)-(3) lower the brush onto the paper, briefly move it downward or horizontally as in the vertical stroke or horizontal stroke; (4) lift the brush; (5) press down; (6) lift the brush upward and turn the tip; and (7) lift the brush cleanly off the paper to leave a neat hook shape.

◈ *请参照下面的图示，按照毛笔的运笔步骤练习，并练习各种变体。*

◈ Please refer to the examples below, follow the brush movement, and practice the variations.

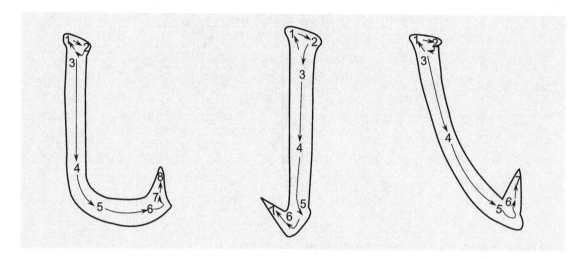

5. 提

写"提"画的步骤是:(1)下笔;(2)向下按笔;(3)向右按笔转锋;(4)从左沿 45°角向右上方运笔;(5)渐渐提笔,直到出现一个尖尖的尾部。

5. The raise

To create the raise, (1) touch the brush onto the paper; (2) press the brush downward; (3) press to the right and turn the tip; (4) move the brush at a 45° angle from left to right up the paper; and (5) as you end the stroke, lift the brush gradually to give it a sharp tip.

◈ 请参照下面的图示,按照毛笔的运笔步骤练习,并练习各种变体。

◈ Please refer to the examples below, follow the brush movement, and practice the variations.

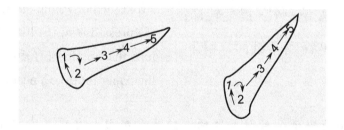

6. 撇

"撇"画古称"掠"。写"撇"画时,起笔的方法与写"竖"画相同,具体步骤是:(1)用笔锋落笔;(2)转锋向右按笔;(3)向左下运笔;(4)慢慢提笔,形成一个像燕尾的向左下的撇画。

6. The left falling

The left falling stroke was called *Lüe* in ancient times. It is constructed as follows: (1) press the tip of a brush downward; (2) turn the tip and press to the right; (3) move downward to the left; and (4) lift the brush slowly to complete a swallowtail-like stroke.

◈ 请参照下面的图示，按照毛笔的运笔步骤练习，并练习各种变体。

◈ Please refer to the examples below, follow the brush movement, and practice the variations.

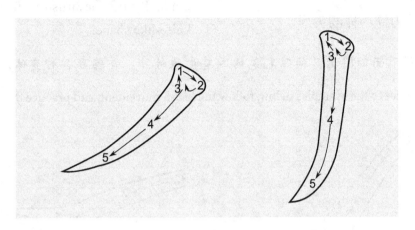

7. 短撇

"短撇"古称"啄"。写"短撇"的步骤是：（1）用笔锋向上运笔；（2）转锋向右按笔；（3）从右向左下运笔；（4）逐渐提笔，以一个尖形的尾巴收尾。"短撇"比一般的"撇"短，运笔快，形状像小鸟啄食。

7. The aside

The aside was called *Zhuo* in ancient times. To create the aside, (1) move the tip of a brush upward; (2) turn the tip and press to the right; (3) move the brush from the right to the left and press down; and (4) lift the brush gradually to give it a sharp tip. The aside is shorter than the left falling, and the brush moves faster. It looks like a pecking bird.

◈ 请参照下面的图示，按照毛笔的运笔步骤练习，并练习各种变体。

◈ Please refer to the examples below, follow the brush movement, and practice the variations.

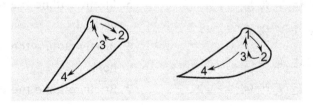

8. 捺

"捺"就是向右下落的笔画。写"捺"的步骤是：（1）在左上方起笔；（2）开始轻轻向右下按笔，逐渐加压，笔画

8. The right falling

To write *Na*, literally "right falling", (1) begin at the top left; (2) proceed by pressing down lightly to the right, gradually increasing the pressure on the paper to thicken the stroke;

也逐渐加重；（3）呈倾斜形地向下运笔，直到右下角；（4）顿笔并按笔；（5）慢慢提笔，形成像刀锋一样的尖形。

(3) move diagonally down to the bottom right; (4) pause and press the brush; and (5) gradually lift the brush to form a sharp and knife-like shape.

◆ 请参照下面的图示，按照毛笔的运笔步骤练习，并练习各种变体。

◆ Please refer to the examples below, follow the brush movement, and practice the variations.

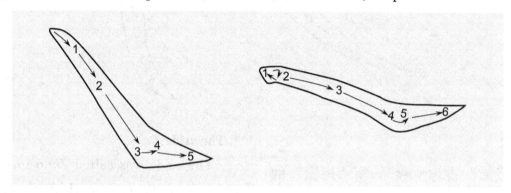

思考题 Questions

1. 哪个汉字包括八种基本笔画？

2. 为什么初学者常常要花费好几个月的时间来练习八种基本笔画？每种笔画都有变体吗？

3. 概述写"点"的运笔步骤。

4. 概述写"横"的运笔步骤。

5. 概述写"竖"的运笔步骤。

6. 概述写"钩"的运笔步骤。

7. 概述写"提"的运笔步骤。

8. 概述写"撇"的运笔步骤。

9. 概述写"短撇"的运笔步骤。

10. 概述写"捺"的运笔步骤。

1. Which character contains the eight basic strokes?

2. Why do beginners often spend several months practicing the eight basic strokes? Does each stroke have a variation?

3. Briefly outline the brush movement for the dot.

4. Briefly outline the brush movement for the horizontal.

5. Briefly outline the brush movement for the vertical.

6. Briefly outline the brush movement for the hook.

7. Briefly outline the brush movement for the raise.

8. Briefly outline the brush movement for the left falling.

9. Briefly outline the brush movement for the aside.

10. Briefly outline the brush movement for the right falling.

第十章 怎样练习书法
Chapter Ten How to Practice Chinese Calligraphy

如果想成为书法家，就需要长期坚持不懈地练习，这不是一朝一夕可以达成的目标。初学书法要做到百练不烦，全神贯注。书法练习看起来似乎是缓慢、枯燥的过程，实际上却要求练习者做到身心的结合，通过自我调控和耐心磨炼来完善性格，提高文化与艺术等方面的修养，所以学习书法是一个可以伴随一生且让人受益无穷的爱好。

10.1 练习书法的基本要求

初学者首先要端坐于桌前，保持头正、腰直、脚平放，练习纸放在正前方。正确握毛笔的方法是直握笔杆，笔锋在书写时始终与纸面保持垂直（图10-1）。虽然这种姿势和方法刚开始时会让人感到不习惯，但它是把字写好的关键。正如庞慎言先生所指出的："学习书法，必先懂得做'五正'的功夫：就是要心正、头正、身正、足正、笔正。这五正的功夫做得切实与否关系到书法之能否有所成就。"[1]

---

[1] 庞慎言（1990）《书法指引》，台北：文史哲出版社。

It is not possible to become a calligrapher overnight. It may take a lifetime of work before one can be considered a master calligrapher. Beginners should be ready to commit to repeated practice and concentration. Calligraphy practice seems to be a slow and boring process, but in fact, it requires the practitioner to achieve the combination of body and mind, improve the personality, culture, art and other aspects of cultivation through self-regulation and patient training. Therefore, learning calligraphy is a lifelong and beneficial hobby.

10.1 Basic Requirements for Practicing Calligraphy

Beginners should first sit upright at a table with your head straight, waist straight, feet flat, and the writing paper directly in front. The brush is held vertically so that the tip never has a slant when coming in contact with the writing surface (Figure 10-1). The manner in which one uses a brush at first can make people feel quite awkward; however it hinges on whether you will have a good practice of calligraphy. As Mr. Pang Shenyan puts it, "To learn calligraphy, one should first of all understand the 'correctitude' of five skills: the correctitude in the state of mind, in the positions of head, body, feet and brush. Whether one can master such five

学习书法所需要的文具不多——一支好笔、适合书写的纸、墨和砚台。一般来说，在开始练习书法之前需要做到以下三步：（1）布置好桌椅；（2）准备好书写工具；（3）学习正确的执笔方法。为了循序渐进地练习，学习者可以先学习描摹，再照字帖临写，最后脱帖练习。

从技术上讲，中国书法并无神秘之处，即便一个孩子也可以在方格里描画出直线、曲线或方框。但是，如果想通过线条的形状和组合带来视觉上的美感和享受，则需要经过长期的训练和对艺术的深刻理解。这一升华的过程取决于每一个书写者的技巧和想象力，不仅每一笔都要写得传神，而且要把一笔一画巧妙地组合起来，同时要求一笔到位，不允许反复涂描。更重要的是，笔画之间要保持自然的匀称和平衡，这就需要长期的训练。一个书法家往往要到五六十岁才能达到艺术上的成熟，才能把字写得得心应手，挥洒自如。正如清末刘熙载（1813—1881）在《艺

图 10-1　毛笔的执笔方法
Figure 10-1　The way to hold the brush

skills determines how much one can achieve in calligraphy."[1]

The tools of learning Chinese calligraphy are very few, requiring only a good quality brush, paper, ink stick and ink stone suitable for writing. In general, one needs to follow three steps before beginning to practice calligraphy: (1) set the table in the correct position; (2) prepare the writing tools; and (3) hold the brush correctly. To practice step by step, learners can first trace the model work, then copy, and finally advance to freehand.

Technically speaking, there is no mystery to Chinese calligraphy. Even a child can fill up a squared space with lines; but to fill it so as to liberate the visual beauty and enjoyment through the linear shapes and combinations, needs lengthy practice and artistic insight. The process depends on the skill and imagination of the writer to give interesting shapes to the strokes, to compose beautiful structures from them without any retouching or shading, and, most important of all, to have a well-balanced space between the strokes. Master calligraphers usually reach their prime in their

[1] Pang, Shenyan (1990) *A Guide to Chinese Calligraphy*. Taipei: The Liberal Arts Press.

概·书概》中所说："学书者始由不工求工，继由工求不工。不工者，工之极也。"

练习书法时要注意以下四个基本规则：

1. 笔画

笔画是汉字的建筑材料，共有八种。楷书中的每一个点、画都有章法，或横或竖，或撇或捺，在起笔和收笔处都要求有特殊的形状，如有些笔画的收笔处要求有笔锋。"点"画也有各种不同的形状。

2. 汉字的结构

每个汉字都可以看成是一幅画儿或一座建筑，都带有它自身的结构、形象、动感和精神。

3. 由汉字组成的字行

按照传统书写方法，汉字沿着竖行由上往下书写。但是，作为书写艺术，字与字之间不应该机械地排列。

4. 字行之间的组合

在传统书法中，字行之间没有太多的组合形式，主要有竖轴、横轴、条幅、扇面（图10-2、图10-3）、对联等。竖轴一般是二、四、六、八组合成对的。汉字一般都是竖写。现代的条幅字数减少，有的条幅只有一个字或几个字，而且从左到右的横行书写方法也开始盛行起来（图10-4）。

50s and 60s. As Liu Xizai (1813–1881) of the late Qing Dynasty states in *Yigai · Shugai*, "A calligraphy student first seeks neatness from the lack of neatness, then advances from neatness to the absence of neatness. The absence of neatness is the extreme state of skills."

Four basic rules to keep in mind when practicing Chinese calligraphy are as follows:

1. Strokes

Strokes, which are the building materials of characters, have eight forms. In the regular style, each dot and stroke have rules. They are horizontal or vertical, left falling or right falling. The beginning and the end of certain strokes require particular shapes. For a certain stroke to the end, the tip of a brush is sometimes required. Dots also differ in their forms.

2. The structure of characters

Each character can be considered as an individual picture or a building with its own structure, gesture, movement and spirit.

3. Lines formed by characters

According to the traditional writing method, Chinese characters are written from top to bottom in straight columns. As the art of writing, however, the characters shouldn't be so mechanically placed.

4. Combinations between lines

Traditionally, there are not many combinations between lines. There are mainly hanging scrolls, hand scrolls, banners, fans (Figure 10-2 & 10-3), and couplets. Hanging scrolls are usually paired

图10-2 明代董其昌（1555—1636）《草书扇面》
Figure 10-2 *The Grass Script on the Cover of a Fan* by Dong Qichang (1555−1636), Ming Dynasty

图10-3 宋徽宗赵佶《草书纨扇》
Figure 10-3 *The Grass Script on a Silk Fan* by Zhao Ji, Emperor Huizong of the Song Dynasty

图10-4 "庆林春茶庄"的牌匾
Figure 10-4 The plaque of Qinglinchun Tea Shop

唐代著名书法家欧阳询对如何练习书法曾经有过很多精辟的论述，概括起来主要有：

（1）提笔之前先有腹稿；

（2）认真考虑书法作品的布局；

（3）小心对待每个字的形状以及字与字之间的间隔，防止倾斜；

（4）墨太淡会影响字的神采，墨太浓又会影响运笔；

（5）下笔时既要避免软弱无力，也不要犹豫不决；

（6）每个字的四边都要相称，部首之间的搭配也要协调，因为一个字的活力和神韵在很大程度上取决于它内在的比例；

（7）大脑和眼睛要互相配合，以便决定书法作品的疏密度和倾斜度；

with two, four, six, or eight combinations. They all consist of vertical lines of characters. The number of modern banners has decreased. Some banners may contain only a single character, or are formed by only a few characters. And writing from left to right horizontally has also become prevalent (Figure 10-4).

Ouyang Xun, a master calligrapher in the Tang Dynasty had many incisive comments on calligraphy. His advice on how to practice calligraphy can be summarized as follows:

(1) Have the idea in your mind before you take up the brush.

(2) Design the composition only after you have thoroughly considered it.

(3) Be very careful with the shape of each character and space between characters, and do not let the characters tilt sideways.

(4) Ink that is too pale will dim the characters' luster; too thick will impede the

（8）一个字的形状就应该像一个体型健美匀称的人。

10.2 练习书法的基本步骤

1. 描摹

学习毛笔书法要有一个循序渐进的过程。从书体上讲，一般先学楷书，然后再学行书或其他书体。从学习方法上讲，传统上常常采用的是摹临法，即先描摹，后临写，再仿帖，最后脱帖练习。

在开始描摹之前，先要做好如下准备工作：

（1）准备好书写工具：笔、墨、纸、砚。

（2）布置好桌面：如果你用右手执笔，就把毛笔和砚台等放在桌子的右角，以便拿放。

（3）磨墨：磨墨的过程也是书法练习前平心静气、集中精神的过程。如果为了节省时间，也可以使用墨汁，但是最好自己研磨。

"摹"，俗称"描红"，就是把薄纸蒙在要学习的字帖上，然后按照字帖的范例把字描摹出来。

描摹法还可以分为两种：一种是按照笔画顺序描写出字形即可，运笔较快；另一种是完全按照范例，细心、准确地

flow of the brush.

(5) Do not write a character with weakness, nor with a hesitant feeling.

(6) Let all the four sides be evenly proportioned and all parts coordinated. The animation and spirit of a character depend greatly upon its proportion.

(7) Mind and eye together should determine density or looseness and the degree of inclination of calligraphic works.

(8) The shape of a character should be like that of a well-built man.

10.2 Basic Steps to Practice Calligraphy

1. Tracing the model work

Brush calligraphy should be learned step by step. As for the writing style, it is generally agreed that the regular style should be learned first and followed by the running style or other writing styles. The learning method has traditionally consisted of tracing and copying the model work before starting freehand practice.

Keep the following process in mind before tracing the model work:

(1) Prepare the writing tools: the brush, ink stick, paper and ink stone.

(2) Set up the table. Put the brush and ink stone within easy reach on the right side if you are right-handed.

(3) Grind ink. The process of grinding ink is also a process of calm and concentration before calligraphy practice. You can also use ready-made ink to save time, but it is best to grind it yourself.

描摹出一笔一画的形状，再现书法范例的原形。

近些年来，有一种更为流行的描摹方法，即采用中空笔画的方法，勾勒出每个汉字的字形，然后让初学者按照轮廓填摹。这种方法称为"双钩"。

下面是"双钩"描摹的例子：

Mo, commonly known as tracing, means putting a thin piece of paper over the characters you are going to learn and then writing the character out according to the model work.

There are two types of tracing. The faster method is to copy the shape of the character according to the stroke order. The other way is to trace every single stroke carefully and accurately, and brings to life the complete features of the model work.

In recent years, a new way of tracing has become common. The outline of the character is traced and then the beginner just fills in the inside. This method is known as *Shuanggou*.

The following are examples of filling in the inside:

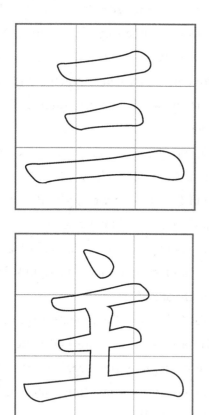

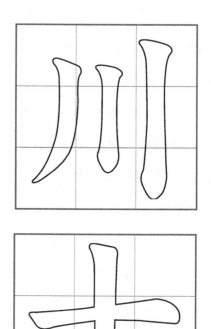

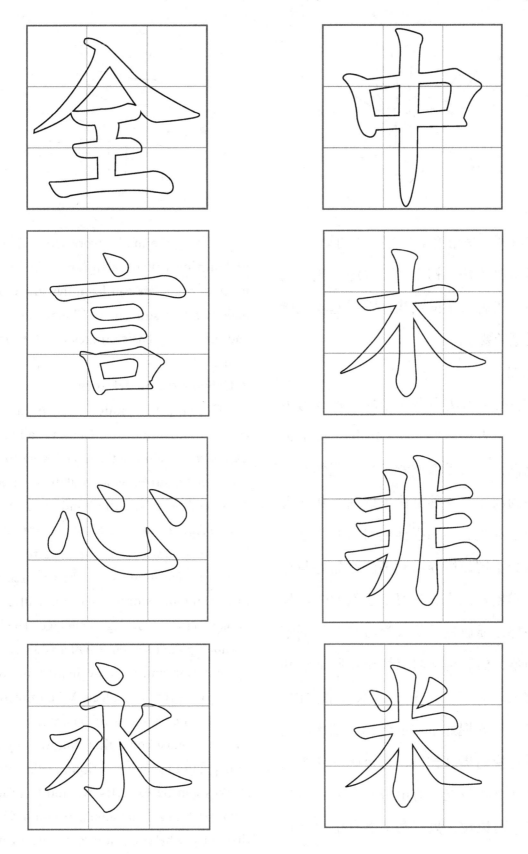

描摹法是用毛笔学习书法的第一步。通过这种方法，初学者可以练习笔顺的先后，了解汉字的结构，掌握基本笔画和运笔的要领。

2. 临帖

临贴是书法中最常用的一种练习方法。初学者要看着字帖，一笔一画地模仿范例，写出近似或看起来与范例基本相同的汉字。这种方法可以训练初学者眼和手的配合，加强他们对笔画、字形结构的了解，培养出对书法作品好与坏的分辨鉴赏能力。学习书法就像学习外语一样，要通过模仿来学习基本的词汇和句型，然后再学习怎样用这些词汇和句型去表达自己的思想。练习书法时，也需要先掌握好基本的笔画、结构，然后通过模仿提高技能，直至能够熟练运用这些基本技能，写出带有个人特色的汉字。可以说，只有到了能自由熟练运

Tracing the model work is the first step of learning brush calligraphy. Using this method, beginners can learn the stroke order, understand the structure of Chinese characters, and master the basic strokes and the writing skills.

2. Copying the model work

Copying the model work is the most common way to practice Chinese calligraphy. Beginners should use the model work to copy every single stroke as accurately as possible. This method trains the hands and eyes of the beginners to cooperate. It strengthens beginners' understanding of strokes and structures and it cultivates their appreciation of calligraphic works. Learning calligraphy is like learning a foreign language. The basic vocabulary and sentence patterns are learned by imitation and then we learn how to use them to express our ideas. When practicing calligraphy, mastery of basic strokes and structures must come first, followed by a lot of copying to improve writing skills until the strokes can be expertly written to produce unique Chinese characters. It could be said that only when learners are able to write

用的阶段，学习者才能够辨别出书法作品好与坏的区别。

在开始临帖以前，要选好字帖，把字帖放在桌子的左边，仔细揣摩每一个要临摹的字，同时认真分析每个字的结构及每一笔的位置和写法。

经过长期临摹某一位书法大师的作品后，学习者可以进入自由模仿的练习阶段。仿品的书写者应签署自己的名字。有时候，好的仿品甚至可以以假乱真，人们往往难以分辨真迹和仿品，这样的复制品称为"赝品"。

下面是可供临摹的楷书范例。长期以来，最受欢迎的书法大师有唐代的颜真卿、柳公权、欧阳询和元代的赵孟頫。他们所创的书体分别称为颜体（图 10-5、图 10-6）、柳体（图 10-7、图 10-8）、欧体（图 10-9、图 10-10）和赵体（图 10-11、图 10-12）。初学者可以根据自己的爱好进行选择并集中精力先练习其中一种书体。

characters skillfully, can the bad handwriting be distinguished from the good.

Before starting to copy the model work, the model piece of calligraphy should be placed on the left side of the table. Contemplate each of the characters that are to be copied, and analyze each structure and the placement and writing method of each stroke.

After copying a master's work for a long time, learners may try freehand copying. The copier should sign his or her name on the paper because sometimes a good copy work can be indistinguishable from the model, making it difficult to differentiate between the model piece and the copy work and become counterfeit.

The following are several model works in the regular style. The most popular calligraphers are Yan Zhenqing, Liu Gongquan, Ouyang Xun from the Tang Dynasty and Zhao Mengfu from the Yuan Dynasty for a long time. Their model works for beginners to copy are Yan style (Figure 10-5 & 10-6), Liu style (Figure 10-7 & 10-8), Ou style (Figure 10-9 & 10-10) and Zhao style (Figure 10-11 & 10-12). Beginners can choose and focus on any one of the styles according to their preference.

颜体 Yan Style

图 10-5 《双鹤铭》
Figure 10-5 *Shuang He Ming*
(meaning "Inscriptions about Two
Cranes")

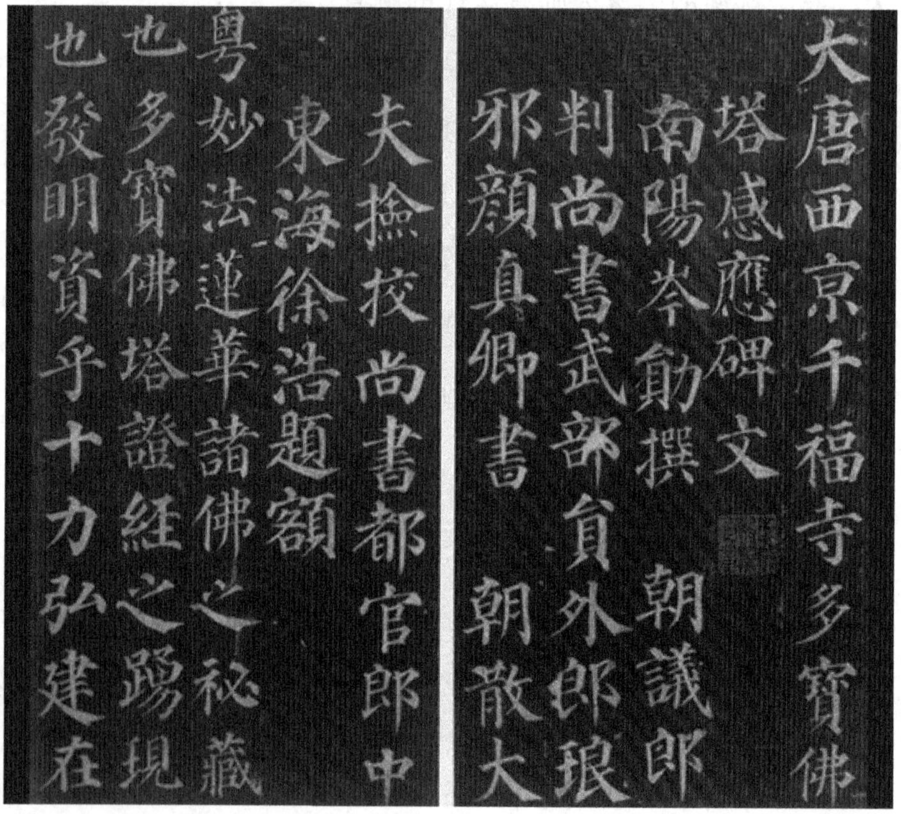

图 10-6 《多宝塔感应碑》
Figure 10-6 *Duobao
Tower Induction Stele*

柳体 Liu Style

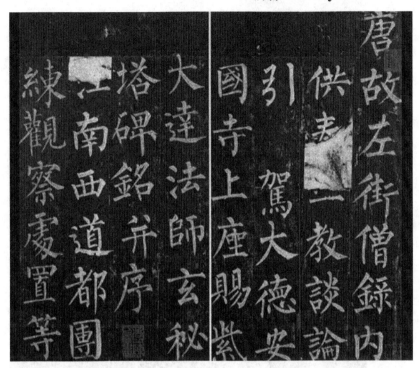

图 10-7 《玄秘塔碑》
Figure 10-7 *Xuanmi Tower Stele*

图 10-8 《神策军碑》
Figure 10-8 *Shen Ce Jun Stele*

欧体 Ou Style

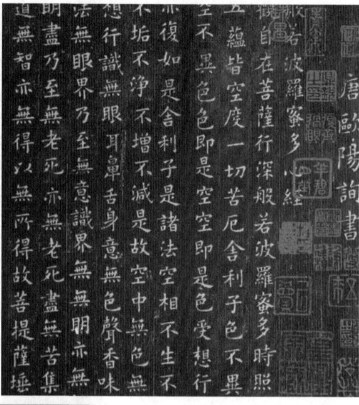

图 10-9 《般若波罗蜜多心经》
Figure 10-9　*Prajnaparamita Hrdaya Sutra*

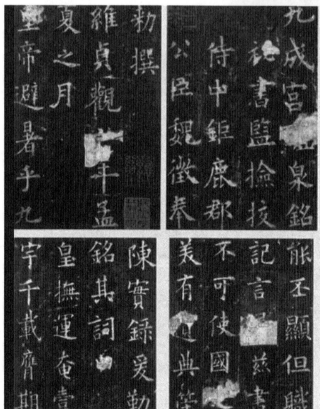

图 10-10 《九成宫醴泉铭》
Figure 10-10　*Jiu Cheng Gong Li Quan Ming* (meaning "Inscriptions about the Sweet Spring of *Jiu Cheng* Palace")

赵体 Zhao Style

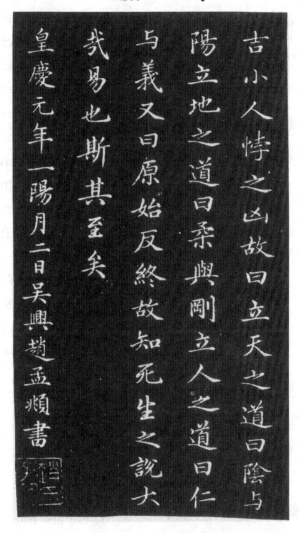

图 10-11 石刻拓片
Figure 10-11 Rubbings of the inscriptions on the stone

图 10-12 《玄妙观重修三门记》
Figure 10-12 *An Account of Rebuilding the Three Doors of Xuanmiao Temple*

3. 脱帖练习

经过描摹、临帖和模仿等阶段的练习后，你就可以开始尝试脱帖练习了。学习者可以根据自己学习、掌握的某一种书体，尽量尝试去创作一幅全新的书法作品，而不是简单地复制某位书法家的作品。学习者可以选取一首诗歌、一副对联，或抄录一段文章，并根据自己的喜好，按照某一种书体的要求及自己对书法的领悟，运用自己所掌握的技能来书写。

在脱帖练习时需要注意：（1）遵循正确的笔画顺序；（2）发挥好运笔技巧；（3）考虑好每个笔画在汉字中的位置；（4）安排好每个汉字在整幅书法作品中的位置。

在书法练习中，常见的毛病有四种，俗称"书法四病"。

（1）牛头：起笔时顿笔太重或着墨太多，结果看起来头重脚轻，脑袋大，身子小，失去了平衡。例如：

（2）鼠尾：收笔时太轻，没有笔力，末端太尖，而中间较粗，看起来虎头蛇尾。例如：

3. Freehand practice

After tracing and copying model works, you may begin freehand practice. Using a calligraphy style that you are familiar with, you should try creating a new calligraphic work instead of copying a calligrapher's work. According to your preference, the requirements of a certain style and your own understanding of calligraphy, pick a poem, a pair of couplets or a passage to write.

When you do freehand practice, you must: (1) follow the correct order of strokes; (2) apply the skills of your brushwork well; (3) arrange the placement of each stroke within a character; and (4) create each character in proportion with the whole of your work.

There are four common errors in the practice of calligraphy, called the "four faults of Chinese calligraphy".

(1) "Bull head". You start writing with too much ink or pause too heavily. It results in the big head with a small body, making it unbalanced. Look at the example:

(2) "Rat tail". The ending stroke lacks strength. The ending part is too thin compared to the middle part, as if it had a big head with a little tail. Look at the example:

（3）鹤膝：两头细而中间粗，或者拐弯时顿笔太重而形成粗重的"接口"。例如：

(3) "Crane's knee". Both ends are thin, but the middle is too thick. This can result from pausing too heavily when the stroke turns, which results in a wide joint. Look at the example:

（4）蜂腰：两头粗而中间细，起笔或收尾时顿笔太重，看起来中间像要被折断了一样。例如：

(4) "Hornet's waist". Both ends are thick with a thin middle part. A heavy pause at the beginning or the ending stroke makes the middle part look very thin as if it could be broken easily. Look at the example:

这四种毛病是书法练习中常见的，但是只要反复练习，就可以避免或克服。

These are the four common errors in the practice of calligraphy. However, they can be avoided by practicing more.

思考题 Questions

1. 初学者应该怎样练习书法？

2. 练习书法时应该怎样握毛笔？

3. "五正"是什么意思？

4. 开始练习书法前要做到哪三步？

5. 练习书法时要注意的"四个基本规则"是什么？

6. 根据唐代书法家欧阳询的论述，一个汉字看起来应该像什么？

7. 初学者应该先学哪种字体？

8. "摹"和"双钩"在传统上是什么意思？

9. 哪一种练习方法是学习书法时最常用的？初学者通过临帖可以学到什么？怎样临帖？

10. 哪些书法大师的字帖是最受欢迎的？

11. 经过描摹和临帖等阶段以后，下一步该怎样练习书法？脱帖练习时要注意什么？脱帖练习时常见的"书法四病"是什么？

---

1. How should beginners practice calligraphy?

2. How to hold a brush when practicing calligraphy?

3. What does the "correctitude of five skills" mean?

4. What are the three steps before beginning to practice calligraphy?

5. What are the "four basic rules" to keep in mind when practicing calligraphy?

6. What the shape of a character should be according to the calligrapher Mr. Ouyang Xun's advice in the Tang Dynasty?

7. Which writing style should be learned first for beginners?

8. What do *Mo* and *Shuanggou* mean traditionally?

9. Which is the most common way to practice calligraphy? What can beginners gain from copying model works? How should beginners copy model works?

10. Which calligraphers' model works are the most popular?

11. What is the next step to practice calligraphy after tracing and copying model works? What do you need to keep in mind when you do freehand practice? What are the four common errors when you do freehand practice?

第十一章　中国书法的书体
Chapter Eleven　The Writing Styles of Chinese Calligraphy

有文字就有书法，有书法就有不同的书体。世界上虽然有多种文字，但是书写起来一般只有正体和草体。除此之外，就是印刷体，没有更多的选择。而中国书法的书体超过十种，比较常见的也有六七种之多。书法爱好者可以从各种书体中进行选择，同时，这种选择也给人们提供了用不同书体来表现个人审美意识的空间，因此中国书法具有更多的选择性、灵活性和表现力。

从中国文字出现之日开始，书法就和大自然紧密地联系在一起。各种书体的出现也是这样。每种书体中每个构形优美的汉字都能或多或少地在大自然中找到它的影子——充满活力，反映着宇宙万物的和谐和韵律。中国人通常认为，从一个人的书法及书体中也可以看到他的内心世界。

中国书法的主要书体有以下七种：甲骨文、金文（大篆）、小篆、隶书、楷书、行草和草书。

It is true that where there is a writing system, there is calligraphy; and where there is calligraphy, there are different writing styles. Although there are many writing systems in the world, generally speaking, there are mainly two writing styles: standardized and cursive. In addition to these, it is printing, and there are no more choices. Chinese calligraphy, however, has more than ten writing styles with six or seven still commonly used. Calligraphy lovers can choose from different writing styles, providing people with more room to express personal aesthetic sense. Therefore, Chinese calligraphy is more selective, more flexible and more expressive.

There has been a close relationship between calligraphy and nature ever since the characters were created. The emergence of various writing styles also reflects the linkage between nature and calligraphy. Whichever writing styles it is, a well-written character in Chinese calligraphy must somehow resonate with the forms found in nature. A beautifully written character will possess vitality, reflecting the harmony and rhythm of the cosmos. The Chinese people usually regard calligraphy along with writing style as a manifestation of the writer's inner world.

There are seven mainly used writing styles of Chinese calligraphy: oracle bone inscriptions, bronze inscriptions (the great seal

11.1 甲骨文

甲骨文是古汉字最早的书写形式，可以追溯到 3500 年以前。甲骨文也是中国书法最早期的形式。然而，直到 1899 年，人们才从河南省安阳市附近（原商朝后期都城殷）出土的文物中发现甲骨文的存在。

在中国使用甲骨文的年代，世界上其他一些地区也创造了近似的文字，比如古埃及的象形文字（图 11-1）、中美洲的玛雅文字（图 11-2）和西亚两河流域的楔形文字。但是，这些文字都随着时间而消亡了，唯有甲骨文经历了数千年的变化之后，仍然能在现代的中国文字中找到它的影子。

图 11-1　古埃及浮雕中的象形文字
Figure 11-1　Hieroglyphics in an ancient Egyptian relief

从甲骨文中可以看到中国书法的雏形和追求。甲骨文和其他汉字书体一

style), the small seal style, the clerical style, the regular style, the running style and the grass style.

11.1 Oracle Bone Inscriptions

Oracle bone inscriptions mark the earliest writing form of ancient Chinese characters and can be traced back to 3,500 years ago. Oracle bone inscriptions are also the earliest form of Chinese calligraphy. However, oracle bone inscriptions were not discovered until the artifacts were unearthed near Anyang City in Henan Province (Yin, the ancient capital in the later period of Shang Dynasty) in 1899.

In other parts of the world, there are similar writings created during approximately the same time period as the oracle bone inscriptions were used in China. Examples include the hieroglyphics in ancient Egypt (Figure 11-1), the Mayan script in Central America (Figure 11-2) and the cuneiform

图 11-2　玛雅文字
Figure 11-2　Mayan script

script of two river basins in Western Asia. However, after thousands of years, all of these ancient writings faded away except for the

样，每个字都呈方形或长方形，字的内部有上下、左右、交叉、包围等各种结构。每个字都由基本上平直的笔画组成，笔画尾部有一点儿尖。字的排列是自上而下，行的排列则是自右而左。这些书写方式都被后来的书体所继承。从出土的龟甲和兽骨中可以看到，刻在上面的字形大多数都很美观，形成了古朴而又高雅的独特书写风格（图11-3）。

oracle bone inscriptions, which can still be found in modern characters.

We can see the embryonic form and pursuit of Chinese calligraphy from oracle bone inscriptions. The writing style of oracle bone inscriptions is similar to other writing styles, which has a rectangular form with top-bottom, left-right, crossing or enclosed structures. Each character is composed of fairly straight strokes with sharp endings and engraved from top to bottom. Each line is written from right to left. These principles of writing have been carried on by the various styles since then. The beauty of the characters from the unearthed tortoise shells and animal bones is apparent; each is unique and elegant while staying unsophisticated in writing style (Figure 11-3).

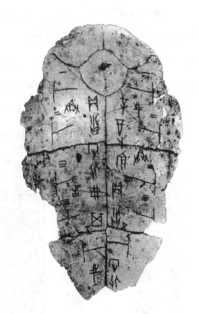

图 11-3 刻在龟甲上的商代甲骨文
Figure 11-3 Inscriptions on pieces of tortoise shell, Shang Dynasty

11.2 金文（大篆）

金文产生于商朝晚期，周朝时（前1046—前256）达到全盛。由于大多出现在青铜器上，比如食具、酒器、兵器、镜子等，所以这种书体被叫作"金文"或"钟鼎文"。与甲骨文相比，金文字体更规范、端正，排列得也更整齐，在"折"和"钩"处更为圆润，笔画有粗细之分。在战国时期（前475—前221），中国分为许多诸侯国，各国都有自己的"金文"，统称为"大篆"。因此大篆字体包容了不同的变体和不同的字形（图11-4、图11-5）。

11.2 Bronze Inscriptions (The Great Seal Style)

Bronze inscriptions came into use in the late Shang Dynasty and were flourishing in the Zhou Dynasty (1046 B.C.–256 B.C.). It is also called *Jinwen* or *Zhongdingwen*, since many of the surviving examples of this style came from inscriptions that were cast on bronze objects, such as cooking utensils, wine sets, weaponry and mirrors. Compared with the oracle bone inscriptions, these characters are more standard, regular, and better arranged. They are more rounded at the corners and show a mixture of thick and thin strokes. During the Warring States (475 B.C.–221 B.C.), China was divided and ruled by many kingdoms; consequently, each kingdom developed its own style of the "bronze inscriptions". The various inscriptions on bronze objects are called by a joint name: the great seal style. Therefore, the great seal style includes variant characters and different forms of characters (Figure 11-4 & 11-5).

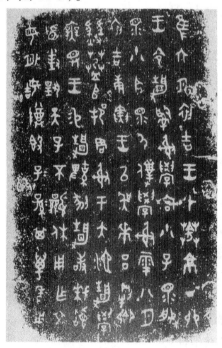

图11-4　西周（前1046—前771）静簋
上面的铭文，大篆

Figure 11-4　Inscriptions on *Jing Gui* in the great seal style, Western Zhou Dynasty (1046 B.C.–771 B.C.)

图11-5　商代晚期的后母戊鼎及上面的铭文，大篆
Figure 11-5　*Houmuwu Ding* cast in the late Shang Dynasty and its inscriptions in the great seal style

11.3 小篆

公元前 221 年秦始皇统一中国后，下令对原有的字体进行修改、规范，以秦国原有文字为基础，确立了标准的字体——小篆。小篆更加具有文字抽象性的符号特征，减少了书体的图画成分，更加强调笔画之间的匀称，更便于书写。小篆笔画粗细一致，无轻重、提按之分。字形变长，因而更适合竖写（图 11-6、图 11-7）。可以说，小篆是建立在大篆基础上的更为完善的书写系统。

11.3 The Small Seal Style

In 221 B.C., the first unifier and emperor of China, Emperor Qin Shihuang, ordered the standardization of the writing system. This standard writing style, later known as the small seal style, was established according to the writing style of his native state, Qin. The small seal style reduces the pictographic elements within the writing system, making it more symbolic and easier to write. It also emphasizes the balance between the strokes. The lines are all of an even thickness and the characters are elongated. This makes it easier to write in a vertical manner (Figure 11-6 & 11-7). It could be said that the small seal style is a better writing system that was established on the foundation of the great seal style.

图 11-6 秦代李斯（前 280—前 208）《泰山刻石》，小篆

Figure 11-6 *Taishan Ke Shi* (meaning "Inscriptions on the Stone of Mount Tai") in the small seal style by Li Si (280 B.C.–208 B.C.), Qin Dynasty

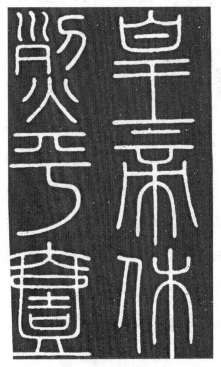

图 11-7 秦代李斯《会稽刻石》，小篆

Figure 11-7 *Kuaiji Ke Shi* (meaning "Inscriptions on a Stone of Kuaiji") in the small seal style by Li Si, Qin Dynasty

11.4 隶书

随着信息交流的频繁，人们写字时自然要求快速便捷，而且富于变化。小篆那种笔画匀称、粗细一致的规则逐渐被打破，出现了各种变体或俗体。到了汉代（前206—公元220），小篆逐渐被另一种书体取代。这种书体用毛笔书写起来更简易，也更流畅，当时见于各种文本，比如税赋、统计、契约等等。因最初为徒隶所写，所以这种书体被命名为"隶书"（图11-8至图11-11）。

隶书的特点之一是横画起笔处比较粗重，像个"蚕头"，而横画的末端向上扬起，俗称"刀笔"或"雁尾"，两者合称"蚕头燕尾"。这样的写法带有运笔流畅、不拘一格的韵味。同时，隶书也追求变化，有时一个字有三个横画并列，那么头两个横画可以写得较短，而且没有头尾的变化，只有最下面的横画要用特别的写法，如"三""王"。再有，隶书中汉字的"拐角"也由小篆的"圆角"变成了"方角"，而方角写起来更容易，也更有力度。这些创新增加了书法的自由度和个性化，也增添了变化和动感，因而隶书逐渐取代小篆，成为当时一种规范的书体。

11.4 The Clerical Style

As exchanges of information became more frequent, people needed to write swiftly and conveniently to keep up with the changes. The rules of symmetrical strokes and uniform thickness of the small seal style were gradually broken, and various variants appeared. During the Han Dynasty (206 B.C.-220 A.D.), the small seal style was gradually replaced by another writing style that could be written more quickly and easily with a brush. This new writing style has been found on official documents such as government records of taxes, census records, deeds, etc. It is referred to as *Lishu* because it was first written by prisoners and slaves (Figure 11-8 to 11-11).

One of the characteristics of the clerical style is that the horizontal stroke has a depiction at the beginning like a silkworm's head, and an upward tilt at the end like the "knife stroke" or a "wild goose's tail", which is known as "a silkworm's head and a wild goose's tail". This writing method gives each character a fluid quality. At the same time, the clerical style also emphasizes changes. If one character has three parallel horizontal strokes, the first two should be short without changes at the beginning and ending strokes and the last one should be written in a special way, such as 三, 王. In addition, the round corners of a character in the small seal style were changed to square corners in the clerical style. It is somewhat easier and more dynamic to write square corners. These innovations

图 11-8 汉代《张迁碑》，隶书
Figure 11-8 *Zhang Qian Stele* in the clerical style, Han Dynasty

图 11-9 汉代《乙瑛碑》，隶书
Figure 11-9 *Yi Ying Stele* in the clerical style, Han Dynasty

图 11-10 汉代《史晨碑》，隶书
Figure 11-10 *Shi Chen Stele* in the clerical style, Han Dynasty

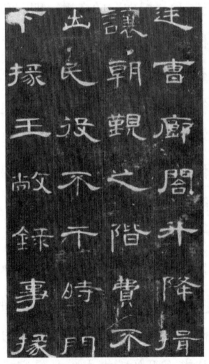

图 11-11 汉代《曹全碑》，隶书
Figure 11-11 *Cao Quan Stele* in the clerical style, Han Dynasty

11.5 楷书

楷书始于东汉末年（公元 3 世纪），但是到唐朝初期（公元 7 世纪）才形成固定的书体，并从此成为汉字的标准字体沿用至今，没有别的字体能取代它的地位。隶书向楷书的过渡经历了数百年，这期间的字体称为"魏碑"。唐朝（618—907）时，从皇帝到大臣都擅长书法，国家设有专门教授书法的学校、书写机构及人员，科举考试中也十分重视考生的书法，因而人才辈出，出现了很多大书法家，他们的作品也成为后世学习的楷模。楷书之所以叫"楷"，就有"楷模"和"标准"的意思，即不仅每个字有标准，而且每个笔画、每个字的结构都有严格要求。楷书保留了隶书的简捷和笔画的粗细变化，但是字形更灵活轻便——横画虽然稍微上翘，但是收笔处不像隶书那样向上扬起；竖画保持垂直，但不像隶书那样在收笔处向外分开。（图 11-12）

由于楷书是中国书法发展成熟的标志，同时技法完整规范，至今仍在使用，所以楷书是学习书法的基础，学习书法应该从楷书开始。楷书也是最容易辨认和学习的一种书体，因而也是最实用的。

have added the flexibility and characteristics to calligraphy and increased changes and movement. Therefore, the clerical style gradually replaced the small seal style and became a standard writing style of that time.

11.5 The Regular Style

The regular style was created during the late Eastern Han Dynasty, about 300 A.D., and became a commonly used style during the early Tang Dynasty (700 A.D.). It has served as the standard writing style ever since then with no other script or style coming close to replacing it. It took several hundred years to evolve from the clerical style to the regular style; the writing style between the two scripts was known as *Weibei*. During the Tang Dynasty (618–907), many of them, from the emperor to officials, became experts in calligraphy. Schools to train calligraphers and the institutions for calligraphy were established and the civil service examination attached great importance to an examinee's calligraphic level. Therefore, many famous calligraphers were produced during this period and their works have been taken as the models of masterful calligraphy by later generations. This "regular" style also means "model" or "standard" script, implying that not only does each character have a standard way to be written, but also each stroke and each character's structure. The regular style preserves the clerical style's simplicity and modulation of line width, but is less formal and heavy in appearance. The horizontal strokes generally slope upward but do not have the final tilt at the end of the stroke that the clerical style has. The vertical strokes are kept strictly vertical and do not lean away from the center of the characters as in the clerical style. (Figure 11-12)

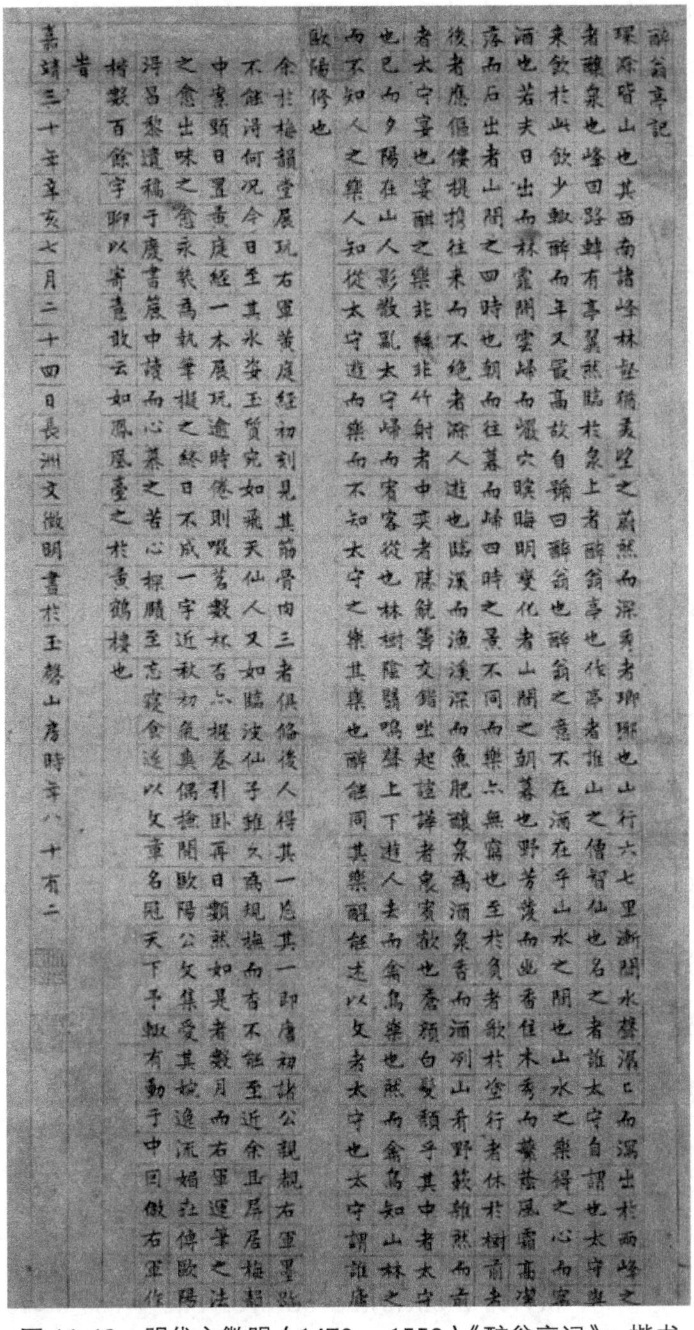

The regular style marks the maturity of Chinese calligraphy with its complete set of skills and techniques. It is still in use today. As learning the regular style is considered the first step to learn calligraphy, students of calligraphy should master this style before attempting others. The regular style is also the easiest script to decipher and learn; therefore, it is more practical than other writing styles.

11.6 The Running Style

At about the same time as the regular style developed, calligraphers sought a simpler and smoother style and the running style was created. In the writing method, the running style is similar to the regular style but features connective lines between the strokes. As the name suggests, this style allows for more freedom and fluidity of movement. It seems as if the brush is running while writing this script, but that doesn't mean it should be written in a rush. In fact, it requires more training and practice to learn the running style on the basis

图 11-12 明代文徵明（1470—1559）《醉翁亭记》，楷书
Figure 11-12 *Zuiweng Ting Ji* (meaning "An Account of the Old Toper's Pavilion") in the regular style by Wen Zhengming (1470–1559), Ming Dynasty

11.6 行书

行书与楷书基本同时出现。由于书法家追求更简易、更流畅的写法，所以

出现了行书。在书写方法上，行书与楷书基本相似；不同的是，行书把笔画连接了起来。"行书"的意思就是在运笔时可以更自由也更流畅，如同行走一样。但是，这并不等于说可以急急忙忙、随随便便地写就。事实上，行书要求在掌握楷书的基础上进行更多的练习。楷书中，每个字的一点一画都是分开的；而行书从起笔到收笔一气呵成，每个字中分开的点画连到了一起，因而在形体上创造出了一种快速流畅的美。（图11-13）

11.7 草书

草书因它的书写方法而得名。由于书写时比较草率随意，不像前几种书体那么规范，所以草书看起来好像纷乱无章，但实际上也有内在的章法可循。与楷书相比，用草书写出来的字在很大程度上都被简化了，在形式上和功能上都带有速写的性质。（图11-14）因此，这种书体往往难以辨认，只有在练习书法多年之后才能涉足。书法家往往使用这种书体来表现抽象的艺术，而不是满足一般书写的要求。

行书与草书的区别在于，行书更接近楷书，同时没有笔画和部首的简化。

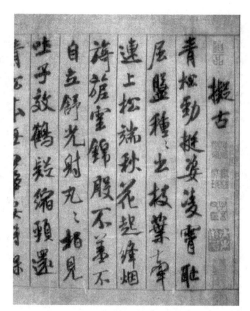

图 11-13　宋代米芾（1051—1107）
《蜀素帖》，行书
Figure 11-13　*Shu Su Tie* (meaning "Book of Model Calligraphy Written on Fine Sichuan Silk") in the running style by Mi Fu (1051–1107), Song Dynasty

of mastering the regular style. The strokes that are written separately in the regular style are joined together in a single sweep of the brush in the running style, producing the beauty of speed and fluency. (Figure 11-13)

11.7 The Grass Style

The grass style takes its name from its writing method, which looks casual and careless and is not as standard as other writing styles mentioned before. The grass style seems to be in great disorder, but it actually follows internal regulations. Compared with the regular style, Chinese characters in the grass style are greatly simplified. It is a style that in form and function resembles shorthand. (Figure 11-14) Therefore, this style is often illegible and can be deciphered only by those who have practiced calligraphy for many years. It is not a style for general use, instead of being used by calligraphers who wish to produce a work of abstract art.

The running style is distinguished from the grass style by its closeness to the regular style and its lack of simplification of the strokes and radicals.

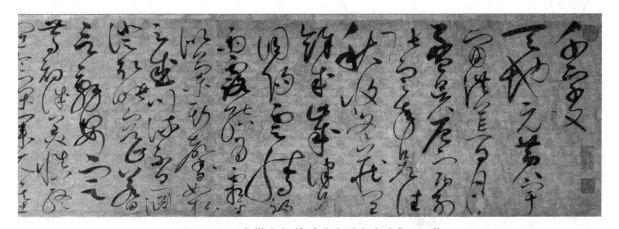

图 11-14 宋徽宗赵佶《草书千字文卷》，狂草

Figure 11-14 *Caoshu Qian Zi Wen Juan* (meaning "A Volume of 1,000 Characters in the Grass Style") by Zhao Ji, Emperor Huizong of the Song Dynasty

附：汉字字体演变表
Table of the Evolution of Chinese Character Fonts

字义与发音 Meaning & Pronun-ciation	甲骨文 Oracle Bone Inscription	金文 Bronze Inscription	小篆 The Small Seal Style	隶书 The Clerical Style	楷书 The Regular Style	行书 The Running Style	草书 The Grass Style
person rén							
son/child zǐ							
female nǚ							
mouth kǒu							
eye mù							
heart xīn							
ear ěr							
hand shǒu							
foot zú							
mountain shān							

续表 Continued Table

字义与发音 Meaning & Pronunciation	甲骨文 Oracle Bone Inscription	金文 Bronze Inscription	小篆 The Small Seal Style	隶书 The Clerical Style	楷书 The Regular Style	行书 The Running Style	草书 The Grass Style
river chuān							
water shuǐ							
fire huǒ							
sun rì							
moon yuè							
wood/tree mù							
rock shí							
rain yǔ							
tool/work gōng							
power/strength lì							
door mén							

续表 Continued Table

字义与发音 Meaning & Pronunciation	甲骨文 Oracle Bone Inscription	金文 Bronze Inscription	小篆 The Small Seal Style	隶书 The Clerical Style	楷书 The Regular Style	行书 The Running Style	草书 The Grass Style
knife dāo							
bow gōng							
well jǐng							
net wǎng							
cart/vehicle chē							
boat zhōu							
ox/cattle niú							
sheep yáng							
horse mǎ							
dog quǎn							
shell bèi							

续表 Continued Table

字义与发音 Meaning & Pronun-ciation	甲骨文 Oracle Bone Inscription	金文 Bronze Inscription	小篆 The Small Seal Style	隶书 The Clerical Style	楷书 The Regular Style	行书 The Running Style	草书 The Grass Style
worm/insect chóng							
bird niǎo							
fish yú							
tiger hǔ							

思考题 Questions

1. 中国书法有几种主要的书体？

2. 哪种字体是中国书法最早期的形式？有什么特点？

3. 大篆为什么也叫"金文"？大篆和小篆的主要区别是什么？

4. 为什么会出现隶书？隶书的特点是什么？

5. 哪种字体是汉字的标准字体？有什么特点？

1. How many mainly used styles of Chinese calligraphy?

2. Which style is the earliest form of Chinese calligraphy? What are the features of this style?

3. Why is the great seal style also known as "bronze inscriptions"? What is the main difference between the great seal and the small seal styles?

4. Why does the clerical style appear? What are the features of the clerical style?

5. Which style is the standard font of Chinese

6. 什么是行书？行书有什么特点？

7. 草书是什么意思？草书有什么特点？

8. 列表概述历史上中国书法常用书体的发展史及各种书体的特点。

characters? What are the features of this style?

6. What is the running style? What are the features of the running style?

7. What does the grass style mean? What are the features of the grass style?

8. Make a table to outline the history of common styles of Chinese calligraphy and the features of each style.

第十二章 中国书法欣赏
Chapter Twelve Appreciating Chinese Calligraphy

12.1 怎样欣赏书法作品

　　欣赏一幅书法作品就像是结识一位朋友。事实上，生活中有很多不同类型的朋友。有的人你可能一见钟情；而有的人你开始接触时可能并不在意，但随着了解的深入而逐渐加深感情。学习者应该和书法建立起长期持久的朋友关系。实际上，一个人对中国书法越了解，就会越喜欢书法艺术。

　　在现代社会，大部分人的生活节奏都越来越快，也有很多不同的艺术形式试图刺激人们的情绪或吸引人们的目光。作为一种传统的东方艺术，中国书法的作用并不在于使人们感到激昂冲动，而是让人们从字里行间去感受一种安详和谐的气氛。中国书法无意与现代文艺竞争令人兴奋的程度，相反，它以自己独特的风采，用视觉上的美感和精神上的力量去震撼人们的心灵。如曲磊磊所说："人们对书法的欣赏程度是不同的。这往往取决于人们对书法发展与书写系统的了解的差异。而书法欣赏中最要紧的是观赏者与书法作品之间的了解与沟通。

12.1 How to Appreciate Calligraphic Works?

Appreciating a piece of calligraphy is similar to making a friend. In fact, there are many kinds of friends in our lives. Some of them will cause you to fall in love at first sight. Others may not attract you at first, but gradually win you over once you learn more about their true character. Learners should have a lasting friendship with calligraphy. In fact, the more you understand calligraphy, the more you will come to appreciate it.

The pace of most people's life is getting faster and faster in the modern society. The art in various forms intends to stimulate people's interest or attract people's attention. Chinese calligraphy, as a traditional Oriental art, is not aimed at exciting people but creating an atmosphere of peace and harmony between the lines. Chinese calligraphy won't compete with modern arts for excitement; instead, it touches people's hearts by visual beauty and spiritual strength. As Qu said, "The appreciation of calligraphy is different depending on the degree of insight into the history of Chinese calligraphy and a knowledge of the writing system possessed by the viewer. The most important point of appreciation is the understanding and communication between the calligraphy and the viewer. It is the spirit beyond the form that is the center of

正是这种超越字面的精神享受形成了书法欣赏的核心。"[1]

要欣赏一幅书法作品，首先就要打开自己的心扉，让书法的神韵与自己的心境交融在一起。要试图与自己所喜爱的书法作品交流，去感受和倾听，并体会作品的内涵，加深对作品的领悟，通过对书法的欣赏达到更高的精神境界。

像中国的各种艺术一样，中国书法艺术的发展源头是大自然。如同一棵大树的每一个枝芽，一幅书法作品中的一笔一画都蕴含着勃勃生机。这与印刷出来的笔画是完全不同的。印刷机不允许每个字的笔画和结构出现一丝一毫的变化，而书法家却不接受千篇一律、一成不变的书法风格。一幅好的书法作品并非格式化的笔画的组合，相反，它像是协调而优美的舞蹈动作，动与静、虚与实、曲与直，巧妙地融合在一起，表现出一种跃然纸面的鲜活的艺术魅力。

一幅好的书法作品往往包括两个方面：书写的内容与书写的风格。好的书法作品是内容与形式的结合体。古人云："情动于中而发于外"，最能抒发内在情

appreciation."[1]

To appreciate a piece of calligraphy, the first step is to open up your mind and let the spirit of calligraphy mingle with your heart. You should try to communicate with a piece of calligraphy that you like and you can feel and hear. Try to understand the connotation of the calligraphic work and deepen the insights of it. It is expected that you can achieve a state of a higher spiritual level through the appreciation of calligraphy.

The fundamental inspiration of Chinese calligraphy, as all of art forms in China, is nature. As every twig of a living tree, every tiny stroke of a piece of fine calligraphy reflects the energy of a living thing. This is very different from the printed strokes. Printing does not admit the slight variation in stroke(s) and structure of each character but this stiff regularity is not tolerated by calligraphers. A piece of fine calligraphy is not a symmetrical arrangement of strokes, but rather, something like the coordinated movements of a skillfully composed dance: momentum, momentary poise, and the interplay of these active forces to show a vivid artistic charm.

A piece of fine calligraphy is a combination of two parts: content and style. Ancient Chinese people said, "Emotions stem from your heart and are expressed in your words." Those characters used to convey such emotions need the most appropriate writing

[1] 曲磊磊（2002）《中国书法艺术简论》。英国：奇科什图书。

[1] Qu, Lei Lei (2002) *The Simple Art of Chinese Calligraphy*. Great Britain: Cico Books.

感与志趣的文字必然需要以最恰当的书写风格来表达。很难想象一个人在不懂书法作品内容的情况下能够完全领悟书法艺术的神韵。

12.2 书法欣赏的六条标准

怎样鉴别与欣赏一幅好的书法作品呢？概括起来主要有六个方面：

1. 和谐

欣赏一幅书法作品的第一步是敞开你的思想，让书法作品呈现出的精神进入到你的精神境界中。大自然是一个统一体，它是由无数部分组成的，如山脉与河流、沙漠与海洋等，而每一个组成部分自身也是一个统一体。书法作品也是这样的统一体。书法作品的好坏取决于笔画的笔力、字的结构和整体布局。这三者是一个综合体，需要和谐的统一。整幅书法作品中的笔画与笔画之间、字与字之间以及行与行之间都要做到协调统一、大小合度、短长相宜、轻重相配，像大自然那样，和谐地融合在一起，形成一个完美的整体。（图12-1）

2. 变化

变化是宇宙万物运转的基本规律，千差万别的事物形成了这个世界。书法

style to deliver accurately. It is hard to imagine that someone can have a more complete understanding of the spirit of a calligraphic work without knowing its content.

12.2 The Six Criteria of Calligraphy Appreciation

How to identify and appreciate a piece of fine calligraphy? To sum up, there are six elements:

1. Unity

To appreciate a piece of calligraphy, the first step is to open up your mind and let the spirit of calligraphy enter your soul. Nature is a unified entity that is composed of innumerable parts, such as mountains, rivers, deserts and oceans, each of which is a complete entity by itself. A piece of

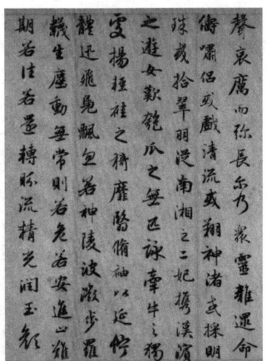

图 12-1　元代赵孟頫《洛神赋卷》，行书
Figure 12-1　*Luoshen Fu Juan* in the running style by Zhao Mengfu, Yuan Dynasty

的艺术性也正是通过错落变化体现出来的。字的笔画和结构如果完全追求工整、匀称，那么就会像印刷体一样，不能成为艺术了。即便是最简单的、只有两三个笔画的汉字，每笔的长短与轻重、起笔与收笔、疏密与大小，每位书法家都会通过不同的艺术形式去表现，从而创造出错落有致、变化无穷而又协调有序的书法作品。欣赏书法作品时最好能与它对话和沟通，尽量去感受和倾听书写者通过作品传达出的个人的心声。（图12-2）

3. 连贯

连续性无时无刻不存在于我们的生活之中，比如白天连着夜晚，春夏接着

calligraphy is also a unified entity. The quality of the calligraphic work depends on the strength of strokes, the structure of characters, and the layout of the piece. These three elements are a harmonious unity. The whole calligraphic work is a synthetic unit, like nature, with each of its part staying together harmoniously and perfectly. (Figure 12-1)

2. Change

Change is the basic law of the whole universe. The world is made up of many different things. The artistic quality of calligraphy is also reflected through these changes. If the strokes and structure of each character look exactly neat and symmetrical, the work would be like typographic printing and can't be called art. Even if a simple character with only two or three strokes, a calligrapher should have his or her own artistic approach. The length of the touch, the lightness or heaviness, the beginning or

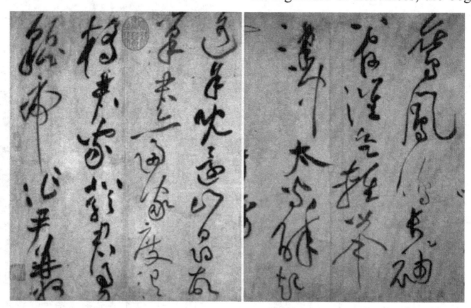

图12-2　宋代黄庭坚（1045—1105）《李白忆旧游诗帖》，草书
Figure 12-2　*Li Bai Yi Jiu You Shi Tie* in the grass style by Huang Tingjian (1045-1105), Song Dynasty

秋冬，事物运转的连续性是显而易见的。这种周而复始、互为依存的连续性同样体现在书法作品中。每个字从起笔到收笔、从左到右、从上到下，都要求互相连接、照应。即使一个字有几个分离的部分，在它们之间也要有连接点。单独的一笔一画可能显得支离破碎，但是当它和其他的笔画衔接起来时，就显得和谐连贯并富于节奏感了。（图12-3）

4. 动感

万事万物都处于运动之中，无论是动物还是植物，它们的生命都在于运动。书法的生命力也是通过动感来体现的。动则有生命力，动则变化无穷。书法作

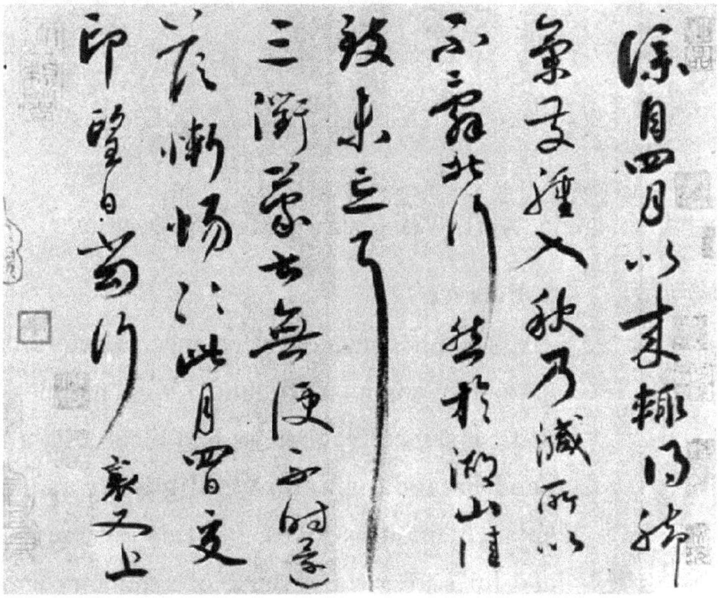

ending stroke, compositional looseness or density, largeness or smallness of each line or dot, all seek to become integrated within the variations to form a unified whole. When appreciating calligraphic works, it is best to talk to and communicate with it, trying to feel and listen to the writer's personal message through the works. (Figure 12-2)

3. Continuity

Continuity exists in our lives all the time, such as day becoming night, spring and summer following autumn and winter. Continuous motion is very evident. The cycle and interdependence of continuity is also demonstrated in Chinese calligraphy. From the first stroke to the last, from left to right, from top to bottom, Chinese calligraphers stress the continuity. Even if a character has several separate parts, there must be a connection between them. A single stroke may appear to be a broken line, but when it is connected with other strokes, the broken line has a spirit of continuity and rhythm. (Figure 12-3)

4. Motion

Everything is in motion, whether animals or plants, their life is in motion. The vitality of calligraphy is also reflected through motion. Motion breeds vitality and change. Chinese calligraphy seems to be a static art, but you can see the vitality amongst the lines.

Motion in Chinese calligraphy comes from the shape of strokes and

图12-3　宋代蔡襄（1012—1067）《脚气帖》，行草
Figure 12-3　*Jiaoqi Tie* in the running-grass style by Cai Xiang (1012–1067), Song Dynasty

品看起来是静态艺术，实际上从字里行间可以看到勃勃生机。

书法的动感来自笔画的形状和连接的方法、书写者的笔力、线条的流动速度，以及笔画与笔画之间、字与字之间的空间处理。动与静是一对统一体，中国书法艺术追求的是"动中有静，静中有动"。大书法家王羲之在中国书法史上享有盛誉，原因之一就是他的书法作品

how they are joined. It is also expressed by the strength and speed of writing each stroke, and the space between strokes and characters. Motion and tranquility are a pair of unity. The art of Chinese calligraphy pursues "tranquility in motion and motion in tranquility". One of the reasons why the great calligrapher Wang Xizhi enjoyed a great reputation in the history of Chinese calligraphy is that his work exhibits not only tranquility on the surface but also an internal dynamic force even after nearly 2,000 years. (Figure 12-4)

图 12-4　东晋王羲之《兰亭集序》，行书
Figure 12-4　*Lan Ting Ji Xu* in the running style by Wang Xizhi, Eastern Jin Dynasty

看起来平和稳健，即便在近 2000 年后观赏，仍然能感受到其内在的气势和动感。（图 12-4）

5. 均衡

均衡是大自然呈现出的又一个常见现象。阴与阳、虚与实、模糊与清晰都要求均衡。书法艺术也要求笔画之间、

5. Balance

The phenomenon of balance in nature is extremely common. *Yin* and *Yang*, emptiness and substance, vagueness and clearness, all need balance. Chinese calligraphy seeks balance among strokes, radicals, characters and lines to create a sense of symmetry and orderliness. A character with a few strokes needs thick strokes while a compound

各部首之间以及字与字、行与行之间保持均衡，以形成匀称、整齐的感觉。笔画少的字，线条就要粗壮一点儿；由几个部分组成的合体字，线条就要细一些，而且每个部分所占比例要适当，以达到紧凑和匀称的要求。汉字数目繁多，每

character composed of several parts needs thin ones with the appropriate proportion for each part to achieve compactness and symmetry. There are so many characters and each one consists of different strokes. Chinese calligraphy, in seeking equilibrium from asymmetry, offers people a feeling of liveliness. (Figure 12-5)

图 12-5 明代董其昌书法，楷书
Figure 12-5 Dong Qichang's calligraphic works in the regular style, Ming Dynasty

个字、每种笔画都不一样。中国书法的艺术追求是在不均衡之中找到均衡，以达到鲜活的艺术效果。（图12-5）

6. 韵律

韵律是事物在连续运动中自然形成的一种节奏和模式。风声、雨声、鸟鸣、

6. Rhythm

Rhythm is a natural process of continuous movement to an organized pattern. The rustling of wind, the sound of rain, the singing of birds, the neighing of horses—each has its distinctive rhythm. Rhythm tends to remind people of music and poems. Chinese calligraphy is called "silent music". The

马嘶，自然界中的万事万物都有自身的韵律。谈到韵律，人们往往想到音乐或诗歌，而中国书法则被人们称为"无声的音乐"。其原因就在于一幅好的书法作品就像一首曲子一样，有着内在的节奏和韵律，它能反映出书写者的性格、才识、情操和心声。通过书法作品的刚或柔、严谨或粗犷，人们可以窥见书写者的性格。而书法家在其作品中表现出来的才识和情操，则被视为永恒的自我生命存在的形式。在欣赏书法作品时，我们要把个人的感受和书法作品表现出来的精神融合起来。无论是楷书、草书，还是隶书、篆书，每幅作品都可以显现出一种韵律，而书法家的才能就是把大自然中的韵律转化到书法作品中去。（图12-6）

reason is that a piece of fine calligraphy, like a piece of music, has an inherent rhythm, which can reflect the calligrapher's character, knowledge, sentiment and aspiration. Through the hardness or softness, preciseness or roughness of calligraphic works, people can glimpse the calligrapher's personality. The knowledge and sentiment in his or her work are regarded as the form of eternal self-existence. When appreciating calligraphic works, we need to mingle our feelings with the spirit of calligraphy. In calligraphy, regardless of the style, rhythm is manifest. The talent of calligraphers is to transpose nature's rhythm into their calligraphic works. (Figure 12-6)

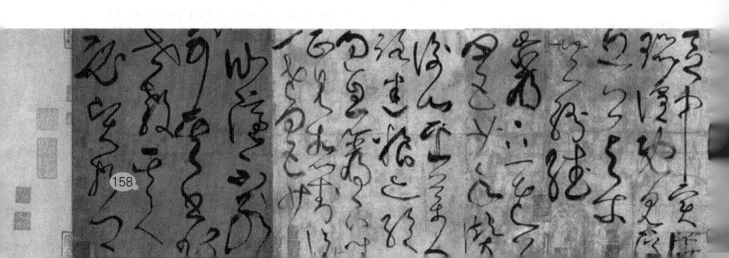

思考题 Questions

1. 你同意"欣赏一幅书法作品就像是结识一位朋友"这种说法吗？为什么？

2. 书法作品和印刷品有什么区别？

3. 在欣赏书法作品时，书写的内容和书写的风格有什么关系？

4. 为什么欣赏书法作品的第一个标准是"和谐"？

5. 为什么欣赏书法作品的第二个标准是"变化"？

6. 为什么欣赏书法作品的第三个标准是"连贯"？

7. 为什么欣赏书法作品的第四个标准是"动感"？

8. 为什么欣赏书法作品的第五个标准是"均衡"？

9. 为什么欣赏书法作品的第六个标准是"韵律"？

10. 你认为欣赏书法作品的六个标准中，哪个标准最重要？你有没有自己最喜欢的书法作品？

1. Do you agree with the idea that "appreciating a piece of calligraphy is similar to making a friend"? Why?

2. What is the difference between Chinese calligraphy and printing?

3. What is the relationship between the writing content and style when appreciating Chinese calligraphy?

4. Why is "unity" the first criterion for appreciating calligraphy?

5. Why is "change" the second criterion for appreciating calligraphy?

6. Why is "continuity" the third criterion for appreciating calligraphy?

7. Why is "motion" the fourth criterion for appreciating calligraphy?

8. Why is "balance" the fifth criterion for appreciating calligraphy?

9. Why is "rhythm" the sixth criterion for appreciating calligraphy?

10. Which of the six criteria for appreciating calligraphic works do you think is the most important? Do you have your favorite calligraphic work?

图 12-6 唐代张旭（714—756）《古诗四首》，狂草

Figure 12-6 *Four Ancient Poems* in the wild grass style by Zhang Xu (714–756), Tang Dynasty

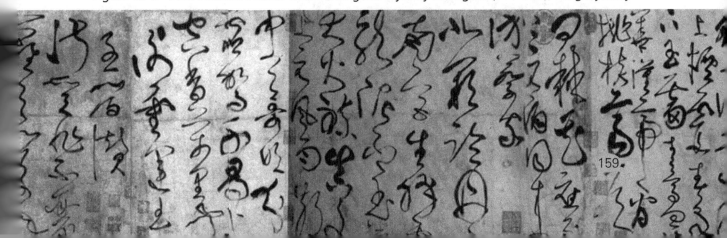

APPENDIX 附　录

Working on a Calligraphic Project 书法习作

经过长期的反复练习，我们可以开始尝试创作自己的书法作品了。书法不仅是视觉的艺术，而且更重要的是，它能展现书写者的精神风貌、思想和人格。通过一笔一画，书写者构筑了每个字的形体，同时也注入了他自身的性格、才识和品味。所以说，书法也是书写者精神和思想的载体，书写的内容和形式往往折射出书写者的精神世界。人们可以通过书法来表达志向情趣、喜怒哀乐。

书法的应用范围十分宽泛，我们可以运用学到的书法技能来做很多事。比如贺卡、T恤衫、碑刻、匾额、条幅、对联、诗歌等，都可以尝试用书法来表现并增添其中的魅力。这不仅是因为书法在中国传统上被认为是最高的艺术表现形式，还因为我们亲手书写的作品，能将我们的情感和志趣表达出来，传递给他人，从而具有更强的个人感情色彩和感染力。

1. 贺卡

人生中有很多值得纪念或珍惜的日子，比如生日、毕业、结婚、节庆或其他重要的活动，这时互送贺卡可以表示祝贺或纪念。如果能够给关爱的人送上

After a long period of repeated practice, we can start to try creating our own calligraphic projects. Calligraphy is not only a visual art, but more importantly, it also conveys a writer's spirit, ideas and personality. A writer can form the structure of the individual character through each stroke and fill the calligraphic project with his or her personality, knowledge and taste. Therefore, calligraphy is also the carrier of the writer's spirit and thought, and the content and form of writing often reflect the writer's spiritual world. Calligraphy can be used to express both people's interest and feelings.

Chinese calligraphy is applicable to many occasions. We can use our calligraphy skills to work on projects like greeting cards, T-shirts, stone steles, inscribed boards, banners, couplets, poems, etc., further showing and adding charm through calligraphy. Calligraphy is not only traditionally considered the highest form of artistic expression in China, but also our hand-written works can express our feelings and interest and pass them on to others, thus possessing a stronger personal emotional color and appeal.

1. Greeting Cards

There are many memorable or treasured days in life, such as birthday, graduation, marriage, festivals or other important activities. At this time, sending greeting cards to each other can express congratulations or commemoration. If you can send a greeting card made by yourself to a loved one, it will

一张自己亲手做的贺卡，意义就更大了。特别是当我们把心中的祝福用中国书法的形式表现出来，那么不仅富有古朴典雅的艺术气息，而且会带上个人的特殊感情，

图1　各种贺卡
Figure 1　All kinds of greeting cards

接受贺卡的人也会从心中感受到这份关爱。（图1）在亚洲国家，尽管时代发生了巨变，人们不再常送贺卡了，但每逢书写贺卡的时候，人们仍喜欢按照传统，书写最能表达祝福的词语。下面是贺卡上最常见的一些词语，可供选用：

be more meaningful. Especially when we express our blessings in the form of Chinese calligraphy, it will not only be full of simple and elegant artistic atmosphere, but also brings personal special feelings. Those who receive greeting cards will also feel the love from their hearts. (Figure 1) In Asian countries, despite how times have changed, people no longer send greeting cards frequently, but when people write greeting cards, they still like to write the characters that best express blessings in accordance with the tradition. The following are some common characters on greeting cards for selection:

(1) 福 (fú, blessing)	(2) 寿 (shòu, long life)
(3) 财 (cái, wealth)	(4) 禄 (lù, high position and salary)
(5) 乐 (lè, joy)	(6) 爱 (ài, love)
(7) 运 (yùn, luck)	(8) 喜 (xǐ, happiness)
(9) 春 (chūn, spring)	(10) 平安 (píng'ān, peace and safety)

2. T恤衫

在T恤衫上印染上各种图案或词语，可作为纪念品，也可作为活广告。穿在人们身上，既亲切又新鲜，使人过目不

2. T-shirts

Printing pictures or characters on T-shirts can be used as souvenirs or advertisements. Wearing it on people, it is both kind and fresh, making people unforgettable. If you can

忘。如果能在 T 恤衫或其他纺织品上用中国书法的形式写上自己最想表达且最恰当的词语，那么不仅能使别人对自己的信仰追求或兴趣爱好一目了然，而且具有个性化的感人力量。（图2）因此这种形式深受大众喜爱，也越来越流行。当然，汉字的字义，字形、书体的选用，书法

图 2 印有中国书法的 T 恤衫
Figure 2 T-shirts printed with Chinese calligraphy

的水准等，都直接影响着其艺术效果及精神内容的体现，也要和穿 T 恤的人的气质和身份等相符，因而需要反复考虑，精心安排，才能在 T 恤衫上用书法起到画龙点睛的作用。此外，在印染方法上也要符合纺织品的要求。事实上，我们常常看到不少书法爱好者利用自己学到的书法技能，在 T 恤衫或其他纺织品上书写出最能表现自我的词语。

由于近年来不少人喜爱文身，所以也常常见到人们把自己喜爱的汉字文在身上，作为永久的标记。但是按照中国的文化传统，这并不是值得提倡的做法。

use Chinese calligraphy on T-shirts or other textiles to write the most appropriate words you want to express, you can not only make others understand your faith, pursuit or interest clearly, but also have personalized and moving power. (Figure 2) Therefore, this form is very popular and more and more popular. Of course, the meaning of Chinese characters, the choice of font and style, the level of calligraphy, etc., all directly affect the artistic effect and the embodiment of spiritual content, and also should be consistent with the temperament and identity of the person wearing the T-shirt. Therefore, it needs to be considered repeatedly and carefully arranged, so that calligraphy can play the role of finishing point on the T-shirt. In addition, the printing and dyeing methods should also meet the requirements of textiles. In fact, we often see many people who love calligraphy often write the words to express their spirit on T-shirts and other textiles by using the calligraphy skills they have acquired.

In recent years, tattooing has become popular. Some people like to tattoo their favorite Chinese characters on their body as a permanent mark. However, this practice is not recommended according to traditional Chinese culture.

3. 碑刻和匾额

在中国的名山大川、亭台楼阁等旅游胜地，人们常常可以看到许多出自名家之手的碑刻和匾额。那些书写在石碑或木匾上的书法佳作，往往起到画龙点睛的作用，和周围的景观交相辉映，给人们留下深刻难忘的印象。比如，江苏省苏州市的文庙内保存着很多宋代石刻；苏州市寒山寺的碑廊陈列着各种书体的诗文碑刻（图3）；陕西省西安市的碑林收存着汉唐两代2000多方墓志、碑石；陕西省铜川市药王山上刻有古代名医孙思邈（581—682）所著的药书。如果登临古长城东端的山海关城楼，则可以看到楼上高悬的一块木匾，上书"天下第一关"五个雄浑的大字（图4）。这些历史古迹皆因名碑名匾而名扬四海。

对书法学习者而言，也不妨尝试用碑刻和匾额的形式来创作。有的人喜欢在

3. Stone Steles and Inscribed Boards

In a lot of scenic spots like famous mountains, rivers, pavilions and towers in China, people often see numerous stone steles and inscribed boards by famous calligraphers. Those excellent calligraphic works on the stone steles and inscribed boards usually match well with the natural surroundings and make deep impressions upon viewers. For example, there are a large number of stone steles from the Song Dynasty in the Wen Temple in Suzhou City, Jiangsu Province. Stone steles with poems of varying styles are showcased in the stele hallway in Hanshan Temple in Suzhou City (Figure 3). There are over 2,000 stone steles from the Han and Tang dynasties in the Forest of Steles of Xi'an City, Shaanxi Province. The medical work of Sun Simiao (581–682), a well-known ancient Chinese doctor, is inscribed on the Yaowang Mountain in Tongchuan City, Shaanxi Province. If you climb to Shanhaiguan fortress at the east end of the ancient Great Wall, you will see an inscribed board with five characters hung high on the fortress building : "The First Pass of the World" (Figure 4). All of these places are

图3 苏州寒山寺内俞樾（1821—1907）书写的唐诗《枫桥夜泊》
Figure 3 Tang poem, *Night Mooring by the Maple Bridge* in Hanshan Temple of Suzhou by Yu Yue (1821–1907)

图4 "天下第一关"城楼及牌匾，
此匾由明代萧显书写

Figure 4 "The First Pass of the World" fortress
and its plaque. The plaque was written by Xiao Xian
in the Ming Dynasty.

自己的书房或客厅里挂上一块木匾，在木匾上书写几个醒目的大字；也有人喜欢石刻，在石头上刻上自己的书法习作。不论哪种形式，都会收到令人惊喜的艺术效果。

4. 条幅

与匾额相比，书写条幅更为便利，因此更适宜作为书法习作。条幅可以直接书写在纸上或纺织品上，以横幅为主，书写好的条幅可以装裱后挂在室内醒目的地方。条幅的内容非常广泛，无论是成语、格言还是谚语、警句，无论是古典的还是现代的，无论是富有哲理的、励志的，还是抒情的、寄予厚望的，只要适合自己或朋友，有醒世明志的作用，都可以选用来作为书写内容。

条幅的书体和字体的大小可以根据自己的爱好和所写的内容来选择。当你把自己精心选择的语句用书法的形式写

well-known partly because of their famous steles and inscribed boards.

To calligraphy learners, you might also try creating your own stone steles and inscribed boards. Some people like to hang an inscribed board with striking characters in their study or living room. Others like to make stone steles with their own calligraphy. No matter which form you decide to use, they will surprise you with their powerful artistic effect.

4. Banners

Compared with inscribed boards, banners are easier to write and therefore more suitable for calligraphy practice. Written either on paper or textiles, banners can be displayed as hangings and placed in a conspicuous place in the room. You can choose an idiom, a phrase or a proverb of classic or modern Chinese that appeals to you or your friend to write down as a banner in Chinese calligraphy. The content of the phrases could be philosophical, motivational, hopeful, or wise.

You can decide on the style and size of the characters on the banners according to your interest and the content. Calligraphy displayed in such a manner can be very

成条幅挂在室内时，你会感到这幅条幅仿佛时时都在跟你对话，提醒着你，激励着你。

下面是一些可以书写在条幅上的内容，供大家选择：

inspiring. It seems that the banner hung in the room talks to you, reminds you of your goals and keeps you motivated all the time.

The following are samples of popular Chinese phrases that can be written on the banners for selection:

(1) 同一个世界，同一个梦想 tóng yí gè shìjiè, tóng yí gè mèngxiǎng   (One world, one dream.)
(2) 欲速则不达 yù sù zé bù dá   (More haste, less speed.)
(3) 百闻不如一见 bǎi wén bùrú yí jiàn   (Seeing once is better than hearing for a hundred times.)
(4) 有则改之 yǒu zé gǎi zhī   (Correct mistakes if you've committed them.)
(5) 识时务者为俊杰 shí shíwù zhě wéi jùnjié   (He who knows the situation is a wise man.)
(6) 四海皆兄弟 sìhǎi jiē xiōngdì   (All of us in the world are brothers.)
(7) 万物同性 wànwù tóngxìng   (All of the existences are governed by a single rule.)
(8) 愚公移山 yúgōng-yíshān (The foolish old man who removed the mountains—with dogged perseverance)
(9) 智勇双全 zhì-yǒng shuāngquán   (Both brave and resourceful)
(10) 天下第一 tiānxià dì-yī   (The best under heaven)
(11) 实事求是 shíshì-qiúshì   (Seek truth from facts)
(12) 任重道远 rènzhòng-dàoyuǎn   (Shoulder heavy responsibilities and take a long road)
(13) 标新立异 biāoxīn-lìyì   (Always create something new and original)

5. 对联

对联一般是指一对相互对偶的语句，上下句不仅字数相等，而且内容相互补充，连上下句中对应词的词义和词性也都相对或相近，充分表现了中文的语言艺术和特色。千百年来，人们喜欢用对联的形式来表达自己的志向和情感。寥寥数语的一副对联，却高度集中地体现了人们的追求、祝愿、希望等强烈而鲜明的意向。（图5、图6）

对联可以写在纸上、织物上或刻在竹子上、木头上、柱子上，一左一右，相互对应，竖挂在大门或窗户的两边。在过年过节、婚丧嫁娶的时候，可以看到各式各样的对联。这是一种深受中国人喜爱的、雅俗共赏的书法艺术表现形式，带有鲜明的中国文化特色。

对初学者来说，选用对联的形式来进行书法习作，不仅十分有趣，而且很有意义。首先要选择好对联的内容，最好是能够激励自己或友人的箴言或座右铭；其次要准备好书写的工具和材料；当然，最要紧的是选择好书体，并书写出自己的最高水平。由于是对联，所以上下联中对应的每个字的大小最好都要相当，表现出对称、平衡与和谐的艺术美。

5. Couplets

Couplets generally refer to a pair of antithesis statements with the same number of characters and complementary content. Words with opposite or similar meanings or parts of speech are usually used in couplets, which fully shows the language art and characteristics of Chinese. Over the course of thousands of years, people like to express their aspirations and feelings in the form of couplets. It is a common practice for Chinese people to choose a pair of couplets that can serve as their life maxim, wish, or inspiration. (Figure 5 & 6)

Written on paper, fabrics or carved into bamboo, wood, and pillars, the couplets should be presented in Chinese calligraphy by hanging them on both sides of a family's entrance door or windows. A great variety of couplets can be seen during Chinese holidays, weddings and mourning ceremonies. With distinctive Chinese cultural characteristics, couplets are popular with both scholars and ordinary people.

For beginners, couplets are both an interesting and meaningful way to practice calligraphy. You should first decide on the content of couplets, preferably a maxim for yourself or your friends; then get your writing tools and materials ready; of course, most important of all, choose a writing style to perform your best writing. Every character in a pair of couplets should exhibit the symmetrical, balanced and harmonious beauty with its corresponding character on the other line in terms of aspects like size.

图5 清代林则徐（1785—1850）书写的对联
Figure 5 Couplets written by Lin Zexu (1785–1850), Qing Dynasty

图6 清代郑板桥（1693—1766）书写的对联
Figure 6 Couplets written by Zheng Banqiao (1693–1766), Qing Dynasty

下面几副对联可供大家参考：

The following are some couplets for reference:

（1）

| 骄傲使人落后 | 虚心使人进步 | Xūxīn shǐ rén jìnbù,
Jiāo'ào shǐ rén luòhòu.

Modesty helps one go forward, whereas pride makes one lag behind. |

（2）

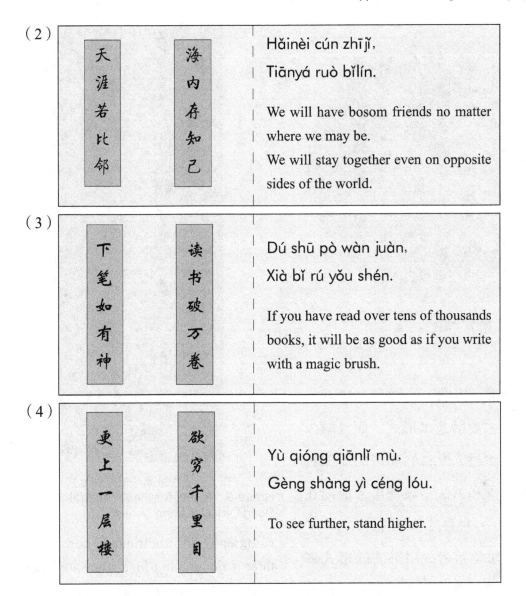

Hǎinèi cún zhījǐ,
Tiānyá ruò bǐlín.

We will have bosom friends no matter where we may be.
We will stay together even on opposite sides of the world.

（3）

Dú shū pò wàn juàn,
Xià bǐ rú yǒu shén.

If you have read over tens of thousands books, it will be as good as if you write with a magic brush.

（4）

Yù qióng qiānlǐ mù,
Gèng shàng yì céng lóu.

To see further, stand higher.

6. 诗歌

中国的古典诗歌朗朗上口，千古传诵，深受世人喜爱。用书法的形式把自己最喜爱的诗篇书写下来，不仅能表达出自己对这首诗的欣赏，而且能使这首诗显得更为高雅、更为感人、更富活力，因为诗中的每一个字都融入了书写者个人的情感和对诗句的领悟。（图 7、图 8）

6. Poems

Suitable for reading aloud, Chinese poetry has remained a popular art throughout the ages. Using calligraphy to write down a poem can not only express the calligrapher's appreciation of the poem, but also make the poem more elegant, touching and vigorous because the calligrapher's feelings and understanding of the poem are integrated in each character of the poem. (Figure 7 & 8)

Since ancient times, poetry, painting and

图7　清代诗三首
Figure 7　Three poems of the Qing Dynasty

自古以来，诗歌、绘画和书法就是中国三种最主要的艺术形式，而且融为一体，相互映衬。大自然和谐的韵律转换成了诗、画和书法中表现出来的内在韵律，构成了一种自然和谐的美。

作为书法学习者，用书法的形式来书写中国古典诗歌，这本身就是一种很高的艺术追求，也是把语言美和形式美结合起来表达自我的最好方式之一。由于中国古典诗歌一般是五言和七言一句，而且上下句之间常常相互对仗，所以在书写时不仅要写好每个字，而且要考虑到字与字之间、句与句之间的空间安排和相互协调。虽然字可以有大有小，但是整首诗书写出来却得浑然一体，诗的意境才能通

图8　明代董其昌书写的七言绝句
Figure 8　A seven-syllable quatrain written by Dong Qichang, Ming Dynasty

calligraphy are traditionally considered the three major arts in China. They are integrated with and complement each other. The harmonious rhythm of nature is transformed into the internal rhythm displayed in poetry, painting and calligraphy, which constitutes the natural and harmonious beauty.

As a calligraphy learner, it is a high artistic pursuit to write Chinese classical poetry in the form of calligraphy, and it is also one of the best ways to combine the beauty of language and form to express oneself. Since Chinese poems are usually composed antithetically of five or seven characters per

过书法形式更深刻地表现出来。

下面两首中国古诗可供参考：

line, a calligrapher should not only write each character well, but also pay attention to the spacing and harmony between characters and lines. Even though each individual character in a poem can differ in size, together they should make an integrated whole. The artistic beauty of the poem can find more profound expression by using calligraphy.

The following are samples of Chinese poems for reference:

（1）

低头思故乡	举头望明月	疑是地上霜	床前明月光	静夜思

Jìng Yè Sī

Chuáng qián míng yuè guāng,

Yí shì dì shàng shuāng.

Jǔ tóu wàng míng yuè,

Dī tóu sī gùxiāng.

Thoughts in a Still Night

by Li Bai

The luminous moonshine before my bed,

It is thought to be the frost fallen on the ground.

I lift my head to gaze at the bright moon,

And then bow down to muse on my distant home.

（2）

明月来相照	深林人不知	弹琴复长啸	独坐幽篁里	竹里馆

Zhú Lǐ Guǎn

Dú zuò yōu huáng lǐ,

Tán qín fù cháng xiào.

Shēn lín rén bù zhī,

Míng yuè lái xiāng zhào.

Bamboo Grove Cabin

by Wang Wei

Sitting alone in the thickset bamboo grove,

I plucked the heptachord to halloo and croon.

The thicket hidden being withdrawn from men,

I was shone on by the full luminous moon.

7. 印章

书法习作完成以后，还可以盖上个人的印章，用这种方法在自己的习作上"签名"。这是一种特殊的签名方式，并且可以永久保留。

治印本身就是一门艺术，需要一定的审美能力（图9、图10、图11）。印章上通常篆刻的是个人的名字，但是它更重要的功能是通过展示个人的审美观来加强作品的艺术效果。中国人认为好的印章可以增加书法作品的价值和艺术性。有时候，用印得当甚至可以增添一幅书法作品的活力。印泥的颜色一般都是红色的。

7. Seals

After you finish your calligraphic project, you can also make a personal seal and "sign" your name on it. This is a special signature and can be kept for a long time.

A seal is also an art form in itself that should be created aesthetically (Figure 9, 10 & 11). Seals are usually engraved with individual names, but their more important function is to enhance the artistic effect of the work by showing the individual's aesthetic sense. Chinese people believe that good seals increase value and artistic quality of the calligraphy. Sometimes, a proper seal can even bring a piece of calligraphic work to life. Seals are usually stamped in red ink.

A seal can be defined in three aspects: (1) seal cutting method: positive print (male) or

图9 清代乾隆
"三希堂"印章
Figure 9 Emperor Qianlong's seal of *San Xi Tang*, Qing Dynasty

图10 清代乾隆
"长寿书屋"印章
Figure 10 Emperor Qianlong's seal of *Changshou Shuwu* (meaning "longevity study"), Qing Dynasty

图11 盖有印章的
《四库全书》扉页
Figure 11 The stamped title page of *Si Ku Quan Shu* (meaning "Complete Library in the Four Branches of Literature")

一方印章一般可以从三个方面来看：（1）篆刻方式，有凸（朱文或阳文）、凹（白文或阴文）两种；（2）字体与书艺，印章上的字体可以是篆书、隶书、楷书、行书或草书，等等；（3）字的布局，字的大小和位置可以有所变化。人们传统上从三个方面来鉴定印章的优劣：气（活力）、情（情感）、形（形状）。

事实上，学习和研究印章是很有趣味的。根据书法作品上的印章，我们可以追溯作品的年代，考证每位书法家的贡献以及作品的收藏者。一般来说，作品上的印章越多，表明作品几经转手，受到众多收藏者的青睐，因而也就越有价值。（图 12）

下面是朱文印章（图 13）和白文印章（图 14）的图例：

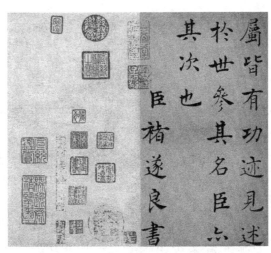

图 12　唐代褚遂良《倪宽赞》
Figure 12　*Ode to Ni Kuan* by Chu Suiliang, Tang Dynasty

negative print (female); (2) style and calligraphy. The style of characters used for seals can be seal style, clerical, regular, running, grass style, etc.; and (3) arrangement of characters. The characters can differ in size and positions. Traditionally, there are three overall characteristics to look at when evaluating a seal: *Qi* (energy of life), *Qing* (emotion), and *Xing* (shape).

In fact, it is very interesting to study seals. We can trace the time of the calligraphic work, the contribution of the calligrapher, and the collector based on the seals that appear on the calligraphic work. Generally speaking, the more seals on a calligraphic work, the greater value of the piece because the calligraphic work has been handed over several times and is favored by many collectors. (Figure 12)

The examples of positive (Figure 13) and negative print seals (Figure 14) are illustrated below:

图 13　朱文印章
Figure 13　Positive print seals

图 14　白文印章
Figure 14　Negative print seals

思考题 Questions

1. 你可以用学到的书法技能做些什么？

2. 如果用中国书法在贺卡上写下你的祝福，有什么特殊的意义吗？

3. 你能在 T 恤衫上用到你的书法技能吗？

4. 为什么中国许多历史古迹上有不少出自大书法家之手的碑刻和匾额？

5. 中国书法适合书写什么内容的条幅？

6. "对联"是什么？有什么特点？

7. 中国书法和诗歌的关系是什么？

1. What can you do with your Chinese calligraphy skills?

2. What is the significance if you can present your blessing in Chinese calligraphy on a greeting card?

3. What can you do on T-shirts with your calligraphy skills?

4. Why are there numerous stone steles and inscribed boards by famous calligraphers in a lot of historical places in China?

5. What can you write on a banner in Chinese calligraphy?

6. What does the "couplet" mean? What are its characteristics?

7. What is the relationship between Chinese calligraphy and poetry?

作业 Homework

设计并完成一幅书法作品。

Work on a self-designed calligraphic project

参 考 文 献
References

1. Chen, Tingyou (2003) *Chinese Calligraphy*. Beijing: China Intercontinental Press.

2. Chiang, Yee (1973) *Chinese Calligraphy: An Introduction to Its Aesthetic and Technique*. Cambridge: Harvard University Press.

3. Driscoll, Lucy & Toda, Kenji (1964) *Chinese Calligraphy*. New York: Paragon Book Reprint Corp.

4. Lai, T. C. (1973) *Chinese Calligraphy: An Introduction*. Seattle: University of Washington Press.

5. Ledderose, Lothar (1979) *Mi Fu and the Classical Tradition of Chinese Calligraphy*. Princeton: Princeton University Press.

6. Lo, Sukming (2006) *Picture Chinese: Art as Language*. San Francisco: Long River Press.

7. Norman, Jerry (1988) *Chinese*. Cambridge: Cambridge University Press.

8. Qu, Lei Lei (2002) *The Simple Art of Chinese Calligraphy*. Great Britain: Cico Books.

9. 陈廷祐（2003）《中国书法》，北京：五洲传播出版社。

10. 何九盈等（1995）《中国汉字文化大观》，北京：北京大学出版社。

11. 罗常培（2004）《语言与文化》，北京：北京出版社。

12. 罗杰瑞（1995）《汉语概说》，北京：语文出版社。

13. 庞慎言（1990）《书法指引》，台北：文史哲出版社。

14. 唐兰（1979）《中国文字学》，上海：上海古籍出版社。

15. https://en.wikipedia.org/wiki/List_of_writing_systems.

16. https://www.britannica.com/topic/language.

鸣 谢
Acknowledgements

自从《汉字与书法》（课本、练习册）由北京语言大学出版社于 2009 年出版以来，汉字和书法教育受到越来越多的关注，有的学校将这门课列为必修课之一，学生选课踊跃。同时，我们从教学中也得到了很多有益的启示。为此，首先要感谢各位师生和读者的关注与支持。这也为本书的编写和出版提供了新的思路。

其次，还要衷心感谢北京语言大学出版社长期以来的支持。他们高度关注读者的需求，认真对待每一份稿件，为国际中文教育事业的发展提供了源源不断的动力。特别要感谢综合编辑部主任周鹂老师在本书编审、设计、配图和出版过程中的精心指导和大力协助。正是由于她和编辑出版人员精益求精、兢兢业业的专业精神和脚踏实地、一点一滴的辛勤奉献，才使得这部书得以呈现给广大师生和读者。

借此机会也要特别感谢美国加州的刘金教授和业界同行的热情支持和鼓励。他们不仅为这部教材提供了很多宝贵的建议，而且热情推荐并积极使用。正因为有了"众人拾

The teaching on Chinese characters and calligraphy has been attracting more and more attention since *Amazing Characters & Magic Brushwork* (Textbook and Workbook) was published by Beijing Language and Culture University Press in 2009. Some schools have listed this course as one of the compulsory courses, and students actively choose and take this course. At the same time, we also get a lot of valuable enlightenment from teaching. Firstly, I would like to thank all teachers, students and readers for their involvement and support. This process also gives us new ideas for editing and publishing this book.

Secondly, my sincere thanks to Beijing Language and Culture University Press for their consistent support. They pay close attention to the needs of readers, take every manuscript responsibly. They have been providing a steady stream of impetus for the development of international Chinese language education. Special thanks to Ms. Zhou Li, the director of the Comprehensive Editorial Department, for her meticulous guidance and great help in the editing, design, illustration and publication of this book. It is precisely because of her and the editing and publishing staff's excellent, conscientious professionalism, and down-to-earth, bit by bit hard dedication, this book can be presented to teachers, students and readers.

I would also like to take this opportunity

柴"，中国文化的火种才得以延续，才能与
世界文明互相融合，交相辉映。

to give special thanks to Professor Liu Jin
from California, USA and the colleagues in
this field for their enthusiastic support and
encouragement. They not only provide many
valuable suggestions for this textbook, but also
enthusiastically recommend and actively adopt
it. It is through the nurture by everyone, that
the seeds of Chinese culture can take root and
grow, merge with other cultures in the world,
and add radiance and beauty to each other.

Chinese Calligraphy
—The Art of Chinese Characters Textbook

中国书法
——从造字艺术到书写艺术 课本

汉字与书法，既是中华文化的传承，又蕴含着中华文化的精髓。这套教材正是王晓钧教授在当前全球视野下传承与发扬中华经典文化的深刻思考与总结。前列造字，后附书法，源流发展，特征风格，所记周详，剖析精切；知人论世，明其品第，智巧兼优，心手双畅；颇多创见，自成完整体系。应该说，这是一部十分难得的开卷有益、雅俗共赏、在美育教学与学术研究两方面融会贯通的中英文双语著述。

——北京语言大学教授、博士生导师　尹成君博士

Chinese characters and calligraphy are not only the inheritance of Chinese culture, but also the essence of Chinese culture. This series of textbooks reflects Professor Xiaojun Wang's profound understanding and commitment to inheriting and carrying forward classical Chinese culture with a focus on attaining a global perspective. It first describes the creation of characters from their archaic to modern forms, followed and supported by approaches to the art of calligraphy. It is a comprehensive series for teaching and learning the content, with detailed and precise analysis, appealing and distinct style, tasteful comments and examples, and creative ideas and analysis on the origin and development of Chinese characters and calligraphy. This series of textbooks emphasizes both knowledge and skills. It is a perfect combination of basic training and artistic appreciation. I would say that this is a breakthrough that integrates both aesthetic education and academic research. Also, it is a rare bilingual book that blends elegance and popular appeal and benefits both learners and instructors.

—Dr. Yin Chengjun, Professor and Ph.D. Advisor at BLCU

欢迎登录北京语言大学出版社网站
www.blcup.com